Silk Ribbon Embroidery
Designs and Techniques

*For Christian, Alexandria,
Rebecca and Victoria,
my very special grandchildren.*

Silk Ribbon Embroidery
Designs and Techniques

Ann Cox

SEARCH PRESS

First published in Great Britain 2002

Search Press Limited
Wellwood, North Farm Road,
Tunbridge Wells, Kent TN2 3DR

Reprinted 2003 (twice), 2004, 2005 (twice)

Text copyright © Ann Cox 2002

Photographs by Charlotte de la Bédoyère, Search Press
Studios

Design copyright © Search Press Ltd. 2002

ISBN 0 85532 948 3

Suppliers
If you have difficulty in obtaining any of the materials and
equipment mentioned in this book, then please visit the
Search Press website for details of suppliers:
www.searchpress.com

Alternatively, you can write to the Publishers at the address
above, for a current list of stockists, including firms who
operate a mail-order service.

Publisher's note
All the step-by-step photographs in this book feature
the author, Ann Cox, demonstrating silk ribbon
embroidery. No models have been used.

Printed in Spain by A.G Elkar S. Coop,48180 Loiu (Bizkaia)

*I would like to express my sincere thanks to my
family, who have always been so supportive.
My thanks also go to my students, many of
whom have become friends, for the challenges they
set me. We have had great fun, they have created
some delightful work, and they keep me on my
toes to develop new ideas.
Finally, a very big thank you to all the staff at
Search Press, who are always so helpful,
especially, Lotti, Roz and John, my editor, whose
kindness and expertise has allowed me to include
so many new ideas in this book.*

Metric/imperial measurements

Silk ribbons are only available in metric widths: 2, 4, 7 and
13mm. Approximate imperial sizes are $\frac{1}{16}$, $\frac{1}{8}$, $\frac{1}{4}$ and $\frac{1}{2}$in. Other
linear measurements convert as follows:

5mm ($\frac{3}{16}$in)	12.5cm (5in)	40cm (16in)	2.5m (8ft)
1cm ($\frac{3}{8}$in)	18cm (7in)	0.5m (20in)	3m (10ft)
2.5cm (1in)	20cm (8in)	1m (40in)	4m (13ft)
6.5cm (2½in)	25cm (10in)	1.5m (5ft)	5m (16ft)
7.5cm (3in)	30cm (12in)	2m (6ft 6in)	

Page 1
Chinese lanterns
*See page 62 for details about making the vase, and page 77
for the details about embroidering the design.*
Page 3
Single rose
See page 71 for details about embroidering this design.

Contents

Introduction

Silk is an ancient and luxurious fibre. It is strong, yet fine, and when woven it has a lustre and sheen that is unlike any other fabric. Soft, fine ribbons are woven out of these wonderful threads and they are available in a variety of widths. The range of colours is glorious and the unique quality of the silk means that you do not have to be an artist or have any special skills to create beautiful embroideries. The very softness of the fibres allows each ribbon stitch to be placed exactly, although no two stitches are the same, so every flower worked will be different. Also, if you want to enhance or change the colours, the ribbons can be painted to blend in with a design, or to highlight flowers and leaves.

I am as much a keen gardener with dirty hands as I am a silk ribbon embroiderer who needs hand cream! I live close to where I was born and my home is built on land once owned by my grandfather. My parents live in the cottage next door and although many things have changed over the years, I still enjoy walking down the lane, through the woods to the river – just as I did as a child. I have loved flowers since these early days and each spring I feel inspiration racing in when the sun shines through the trees on to carpets of bluebells, anemones, celandines and primroses. As I see them nestling on the ground I want to capture their translucent colours and shapes with silk ribbon.

The ideas and techniques which appeared in my first book are developed further in this book, with templates, lots of advice and clear step-by-step photographs. I also show how to add depth to an embroidery by painting the fabric background, and how to colour the ribbon before you start or to shade the petals after the flower has been embroidered. As you work through the projects on the following pages, you will learn how important it is to look at flowers and to study their shapes: how petals curl and change colour, how the leaves fall and much more. Each project is designed to give you inspiration and to encourage you to experiment. All I would ask is that you always remember the following: it is the details that you don't notice at first, e.g. the calyx, number and shape of the stamens or how a stem bends, that will make your work memorable. Happy stitching.

Opposite
A spray of chrysanthemums in beautiful autumn shades worked with 2mm and 4mm wide silk ribbon. The petals are worked in ribbon stitch, straight stitch and straight stitch loops to create the three-dimensional effect.
See page 78 for details of embroidering this design.

Materials

To start, all you need is some silk ribbon, a piece of fabric to work on, a few chenille needles, a pair of scissors and an embroidery frame. These items are all readily available at good needlework suppliers, but to find a full range of silk ribbon you may need to go to the larger outlets, or use a mail order supplier. I have also included details of other items, used for some of the finished embroideries in this book, that you may want to add to your workbox.

Ribbons

Pure silk ribbon is available in a magnificent range of colours and four different widths: 2, 4, 7 and 13mm. All widths are a delight to work with. When threaded into a needle, the softness of the silk ribbon allows traditional embroidery stitches to be worked in exactly the same way as thread. Each ribbon stitch covers more fabric than embroidery threads, so designs develop more rapidly.

Silk is a natural fibre, so ribbons are easy to paint, both before and after they have been embroidered. This attribute allows you to expand the range of colours, and produce all of the subtle shades that are so characteristic of flowers in nature.

Silk is delicate, and it can snag easily, so store the ribbon neatly and handle it carefully.

Silk ribbon is available in four widths: 2, 4, 7 and 13mm.

These irises, shown full size, have each been worked with a different width ribbon.

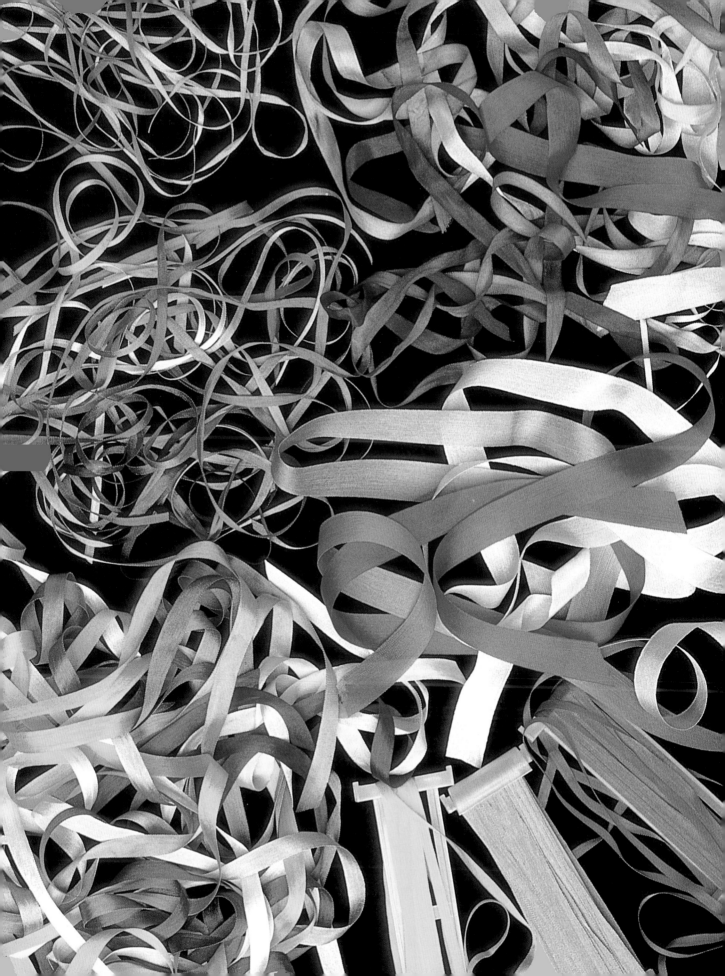

Fabrics

Silk ribbon can be used to embroider any fabric that allows the needle to pass easily through. Silk is a natural fibre and is particularly compatible with all other fabrics of natural fibres such as: silk, linen, cotton and wool, even leather if you make a hole first with an awl or a large needle may be used. A fabric made from a natural fibre is also easier to paint and on the following pages I show you how lightly painting the fabric background first will add a whole new dimension to your work.

Embroidery frames

To work a project you will need an embroidery frame to keep the fabric taut as you stitch. I have found that round plastic flexi hoops are invaluable; each time the ribbon is pulled through, the fabric tends to loosen and it can be easily pulled to tighten it. Remove the fabric from the frame when not working the embroidery to prevent it stretching round the edge. For larger embroideries adjustable wooden frames (square and rectangular) are ideal and the fabric is secured with silk pins (illustrated). The fabric generally stays on this frame until the embroidery is complete. It is therefore advisable to tack a piece of waste fabric, all round, over the edge of the fabric and the wood frame to prevent the edge of the fabric becoming soiled as it is worked.

Needles

Only chenille needles, with their large eye and sharp point, are used for ribbon embroidery. It is important to use the correct size of needle for the width of ribbon being used, to make a hole large enough to allow the ribbon to pass easily through without causing damage to the ribbon. The very large size 13 chenille needle is used for the widest 13mm ribbon. The medium size 18 chenille needle is used for both the 7 and 4mm wide ribbon and the smallest size 24 chenille needle for the narrowest 2mm wide ribbon. A fine size 8 crewel needle is ideal for embroidery threads.

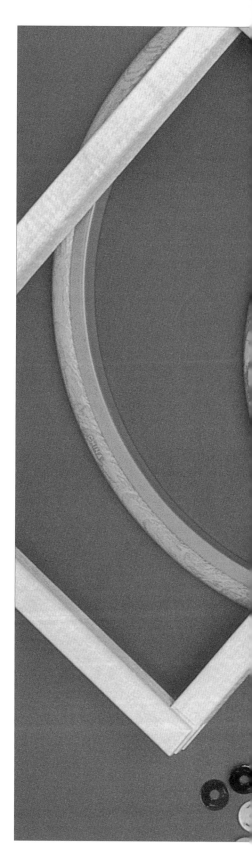

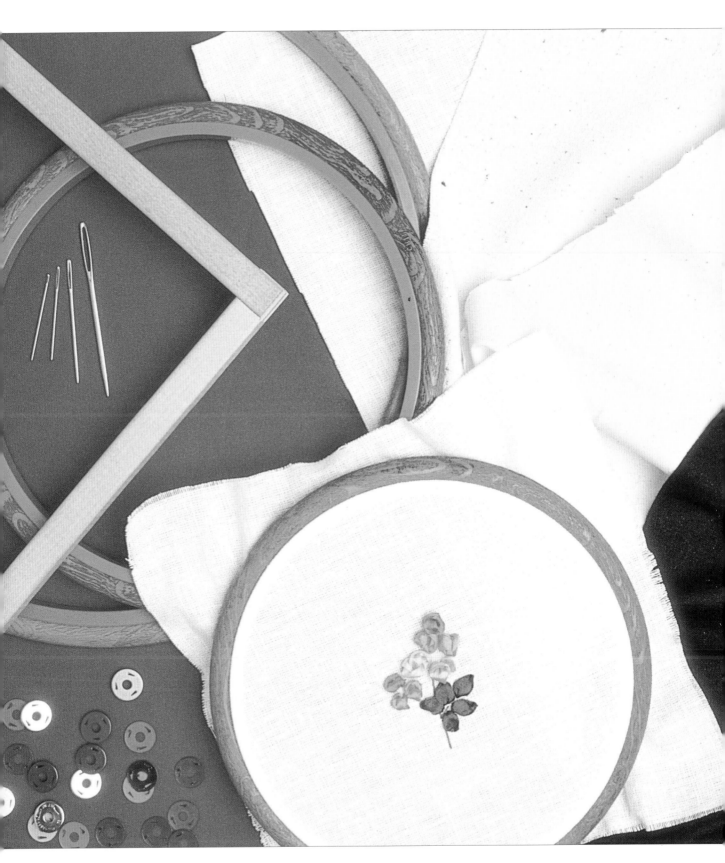

Other embroidery equipment

Apart from the basics, there are a few other items that you will need to get started. You may already have some of them in your workbox, and you can gradually collect others as you progress.

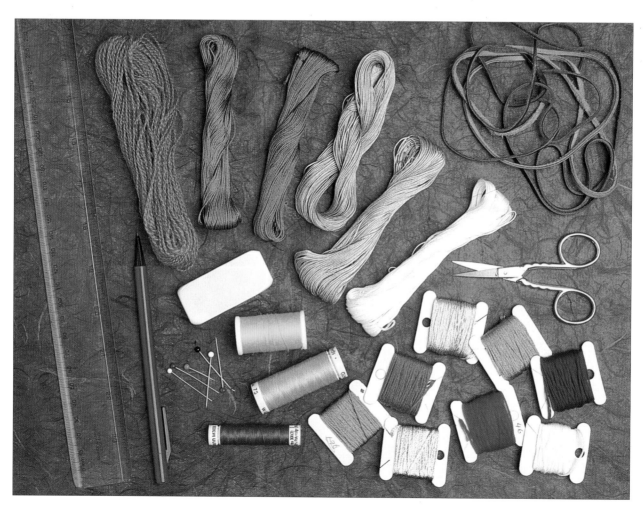

Scissors small, fine sharp scissors are essential for cutting silk ribbon. You will also need a pair of fabric scissors and a pair of paper scissors for cutting out templates.

Pencil and ruler to measure patterns and to transfer designs on to fabric.

Sewing cotton to tack the outline of the templates (avoid deep colours).

Embroidery threads Use one strand of toning embroidery thread to anchor the ribbons. I also mix strands of two or more colours together to make shaded stems and stamens. Different thickness threads, such as coton à broder, cotton perle and fine silk, and different textures: wool, soft string and leather laces are also invaluable in your workbox.

Interesting fabrics I like to collect interesting pieces of fabric, such as lace, leather, suede, satin and muslin, either to embroider or appliqué.

Fabric eraser useful if a pencil mark is incorrectly placed.

Dressmaker's pins to fix templates to the fabric and to anchor threads.

Painting equipment

Painting a background, or altering the tone of the ribbon for a particular flower will bring your picture to life. Painted fabrics and ribbons are washable if you follow the instructions and iron-fix the fabric paints when they are dry.

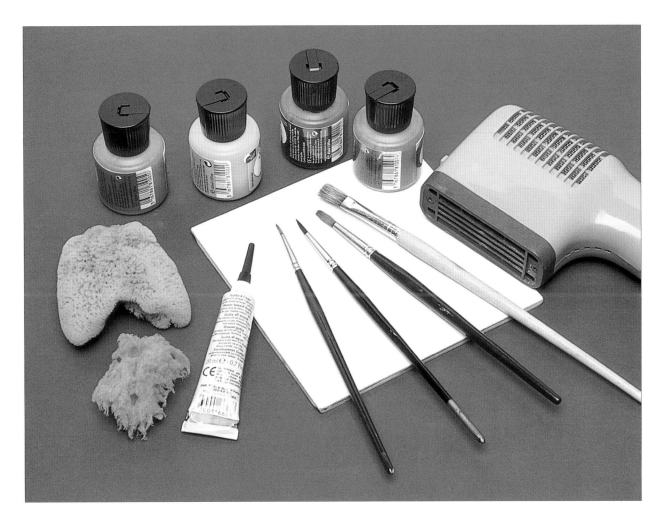

Paints I use silk paints for painting silk ribbons and silk fabrics, and fabric paints for other types of fabric.

Palette I use a white ceramic tile, which has the perfect surface for mixing paints on.

Paint brushes I use a selection of brushes, including a coarse, flat-edged brush and a fine, pointed, round brush.

Sponges Pieces of natural sponge with a different texture are useful for leafy backgrounds.

Gutta used to outline a shape; if the line is unbroken the applied colour will be contained within the shape. Gutta comes in several colours and clear. Mix a touch of paint with clear gutta and you can create highlights on petals and leaves without fear of the colour running.

Hairdryer useful for speeding up drying times, and to stop a colour travelling more than you wish.

Tip

Using fabric paint on silk and silk paints on other fabrics will create different effects, but do test your ideas first.

Polyanthus
(straight stitch)

Garrya elliptica
(lazy daisy stitch)

Chinese lantern
(ribbon stitch)

Rose spray
(French knot)

Anemone
(gathering)

14

Basic techniques

Before you start stitching, there are a few simple, but essential, techniques that you need to become familiar with to get the maximum effect from silk ribbon embroidery.

Preparing the ribbon

Silk ribbon is quite strong, but its structure deteriorates slightly each time it passes through the fabric, so always work with short lengths – 33cm or less is ideal.

Use small, sharp scissors to cut the ribbon at an angle; this will help prevent fraying and make threading the needle much easier.

Although it is not always necessary to remove any creases, pulling the ribbon under a medium hot iron will increase the lustre of the ribbon.

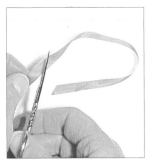

Cut each end of a length of ribbon at an angle of approximately 45°.

Smooth the ribbon by pulling it under a medium hot iron.

Working the needle

To make the most of the silk ribbon it is important to keep the full width of the ribbon on the front of the fabric. It is essential that the needle is taken right through the fabric every time a stitch is worked.

Take the needle completely through the fabric (as for a stab stitch), then carefully tweak the ribbon through the fabric until the exact shape is acquired.

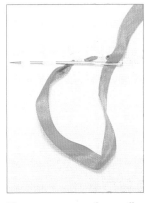

Never try to pass the needle through the fabric more than once, the ribbon will roll and create a tubular effect making it impossible to control.

Opposite
Garden flowers

This charming little garden scene, on a 20 x 25cm piece of pale green cotton fabric, is worked with the basic stitches shown on the following pages.

Anchoring the ribbon

The end of 2 and 4mm wide ribbons can be anchored at the back of the fabric with a knot, but 7 and 13mm wide ribbons should be taken down through the fabric, then anchored with a strand of embroidery thread behind the first stitch to be worked.

Fasten off all widths of ribbon with a strand of toning embroidery thread, sewing a few small stitches into the back of the last stitch worked with ribbon.

2 and 4mm ribbon

1. Tie a loose knot in the end of the ribbon.

2. Tighten the knot by sliding the flat length of ribbon between your finger and thumb.

3. Using chenille needles Nos. 24 and 18 respectively for the 2 and 4mm ribbons, bring the ribbon up through the fabric to leave the knot on the underside.

7 and 13mm ribbon

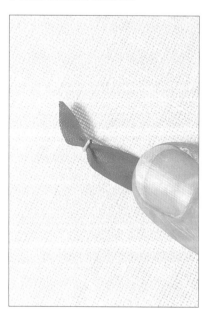

1. To anchor 7 and 13mm ribbon, use chenille needles Nos. 18 and 13 respectively. Thread a short length of the ribbon into the needle, place the needle through the fabric from the right side, then, holding the long end of the ribbon with your finger, pull the short end through to the underside of the fabric.

2. Turn the fabric over, lay the short end of the ribbon behind where the first stitch is to be worked, then, using one strand of toning embroidery thread, secure it with a few small stitches. For clarity, a contrasting tone of thread has been used for this photograph.

Turning the ribbon

Having anchored the ribbon, turn the fabric over to the front and look at the shape of the ribbon where it comes through the needle hole. The ribbon will be compressed at this point and its edges will either curl downwards, in a convex shape or upwards in a concave shape. Sometimes it may even be folded. However, you can easily turn the ribbon as shown.

This will happen whenever the ribbon is brought through the fabric, so turning the ribbon will become a habit.

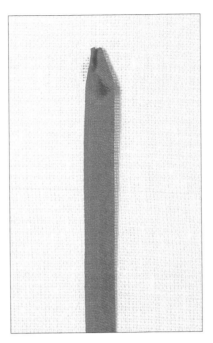

This ribbon has a concave shape.

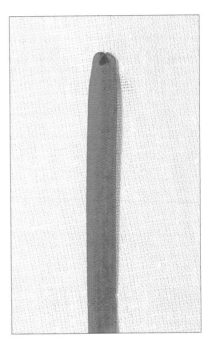

This ribbon has a convex shape.

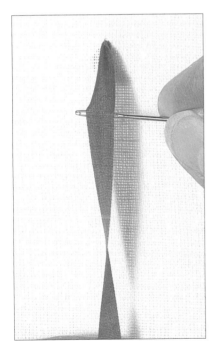

To change the shape of the ribbon at the anchor point, start by turning the ribbon over with the eye end of a second needle (left). Now, holding the ribbon down on the fabric with a finger, and with the needle flat against the underside of the ribbon, slide the needle up the ribbon (as though ironing it) back to the anchoring point (right).

Tip

When working with wide ribbon, especially 13mm ribbon, it may become twisted on the underside of the fabric. Such twists are not visible from the front, but they may affect subsequent shapes. Make a habit of turning these with a needle as shown here.

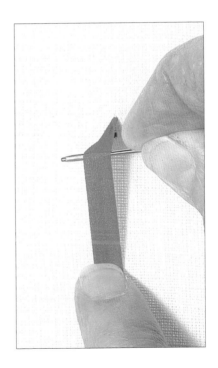

Straight Stitch

This is the simplest stitch, but it does have many variations. It is important to remember that the ribbon behaves differently at the point where it comes up through the fabric to that where it goes back down. This fact determines whether petals are stitched from the centre out to the tip, or from the tip into the centre. Straight stitches may be flat, twisted or looped, but they are always controlled over the eye of a second needle to create the shape required for a particular flower.

Buttercup

7mm, deep yellow (15) ribbon is used to make the six petals of this flower. Each petal is a straight stitch, made with a slight loop that lies just above the surface of the fabric. The flower centre is filled with French knots (see page 28), worked with two shades of soft green embroidery thread. More French knots, worked with deep yellow thread, create the stamens.

Full-size template

1. Anchor the ribbon at the edge of the circle opposite point A and flatten it (see page 17). Holding the ribbon over the eye of the second needle, take the threaded needle down through at point A.

2. Keeping the ribbon flat and tight over the eye of the second needle, pull the ribbon through to the back of the fabric.

3. Leave the loop just off the surface, to give a softly rounded edge, then bring the needle up at the edge of the circle opposite point B to start the next stitch.

4. Working round the design, repeat steps 1 to 3 to make petals C, D, E and F. Keep the ribbon flat over the second needle and any twists in the ribbon will disappear as it is pulled through to the back of the fabric.

Tip

Work the petals in order around the centre shape to avoid passing the ribbon across the centre of the flower at the back of the fabric. Stitching through ribbons on the underside of the fabric will distort the petals.

5. When all petals have been stitched, turn the work over, trim off the excess ribbon, then fasten off the tail with one strand of yellow thread.

6. Use two strands of embroidery thread (one from each shade of green) to fill the flower centre with two-loop French knots (see page 28).

7. Use one strand of deep yellow thread to stitch one-loop French knot stamens randomly round the centre of the flower.

Aster

The narrow petals of this flower are worked with 2mm, purple (177) ribbon. The petals have slightly pointed tips – to create these the needle is brought up at the point of each petal and taken back down at the centre. The centre of the flower is filled with French knots (see page 28), and worked with two shades of yellow embroidery thread.

When there are lots of petals to stitch, start by working round the centre, stitching petals A, B, C and D, then fill in gaps.

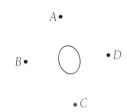

Full size template.

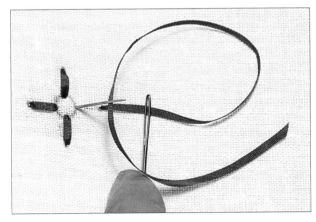

1. Knot the ribbon and bring the needle up at point A. Hold the ribbon flat with a second needle, then take it down at the edge of the circle for the first petal. Repeat this step at points B, C and D.

2. Now work a petal halfway between petals D and A, then one petal either side to complete the first segment. The petals should radiate out from the centre like sunrays, not at odd angles.

3. Working round the flower, repeat step 2 for the other segments. Fasten off, then, using one strand each of two shades of yellow fill the centre of the flower with one-loop French knots.

Tip
Use two or more strands of different shades for stamens to create a more realistic effect.

Morning glory

This flower is stitched in much the same way as the buttercup on page 18. However, the flower centre is much smaller and the shape is more trumpet-like. The petals are loops of ribbon, roughly twice the length of the actual stitch. Morning glory flowers come in many colours, but, here, I have used a 7mm delph blue (117) ribbon. I used white stranded cotton, twisted back on itself, to make the stamen.

D •   • C

E •   O
              • B
         • A

Full-size template

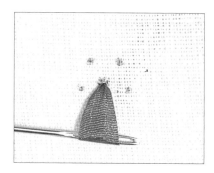

1. Take the ribbon down through the fabric at the edge of the centre circle and anchor it opposite point A. Controlling the ribbon over the eye of another needle, take the ribbon down through point A and create a loop not more than twice the length of the marked stitch.

2. Bring the needle up at the centre circle, just to one side of the first stitch, then down through point B. Make another loop, then work the remaining petals round in order.

3. Now make the stamen. Thread two strands of white cotton into a crewel needle, bring the needle up through the centre of the flower, then twist the thread until it starts to twist back on itself.

4. Holding the loop of twisted thread taut over a second needle, take the first needle back through the centre of the flower.

5. Pull the loop of twisted thread to the required length, then fasten off on the back of the fabric to complete the flower.

Monarda (Bergamot)

This is an attractive and interesting flower, that has randomly placed petals creating its thistle shape. 2mm, deep pink (128) ribbon is used for all petals, and the ribbon is twisted once or twice as each petal is stitched. The shape of the calyx is formed with a fly stitch, worked with two strands of pale green thread, which is then filled with a few straight stitches.

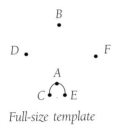

Full-size template

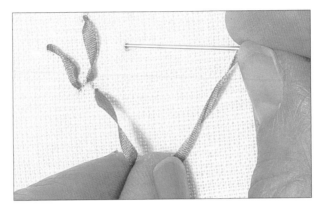

1. Knot the ribbon and bring it up through point A. Twist the ribbon once or twice then, keeping the tension loose, take it down through point B. Bring the needle up at point C, twist the ribbon and take it back down at point D. Repeat this step for another petal through points E and F.

2. Now work all the petals in between, varying the length of each stitch to give a ragged effect. Use two strands of pale green thread to work a fly-stitch calyx across points C and E, then fill the centre of the calyx with a few straight stitches.

Begonia

The main flower consists of fifteen, straight-stitch loops. Referring to the template, the first set of petals are made on the dots, the second set on the short line between the dots, and the third on the long lines. Two shades of 7mm ribbon, bright pink (25) and mid pink (24), are used to create a full-blown effect. 7mm, deep green (21) ribbon is used for the leaves.

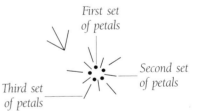

First set of petals

Second set of petals

Third set of petals

Full-size template

1. Bring the bright pink ribbon up through one of the dots. Work a straight-stitch loop over a second needle and take the ribbon down close to where it came up. Pull the ribbon to make the loop slightly longer than its width. Work four more loops round the centre.

2. Now, still using the bright pink ribbon, work a set of slightly longer, but flatter, loops over the short lines shown on the template, then fasten off.

3. Next, use the mid pink ribbon to work five more petals between each of the last petals over the length of the long lines on the template. Use the same ribbon to work three straight stitches for the bud, bringing the needle up at the bottom of each petal and down at its tip.

4. Each leaf is a 3cm gathered length (plus anchoring ends) of deep green ribbon (see page 34). Anchor the knotted end of the ribbon, lightly gather it and anchor the other end through the same point. Stab stitch the gathered selvedges together to form the vein of the fan-shaped leaf.

Delphinium

This tall majestic flower can be worked in many shades and can be particularly attractive when the ribbons are painted (see page 64). For this example, green coton à broder forms the stem, then 7mm, mid blue (126) ribbon is used for the florets on either side.

Each floret is a straight stitch loop, pulled down in the centre by a French knot. This knot causes the ribbon to twist, making the floret more realistic. The florets gradually become smaller from the bottom upwards. You could work the smaller florets with narrower ribbon, but, here, the emphasis is on varying the tension of the ribbon and 7mm ribbon is used throughout.

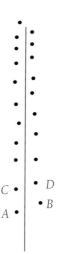

Full-size template

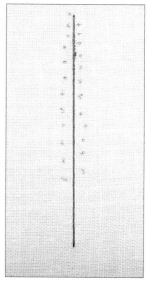

1. Use the green cotton perle to make a single straight stitch for the stem. Do not fasten off this thread yet; bring it through to the front, outside of the image area, then anchor the needle in the fabric, and wind the thread round the needle two or three times to anchor it.

> ### Tip
> As the petal stitches are worked up the stem, the thread slackens. When all the florets have been worked, re-tension the stem thread and fasten off.

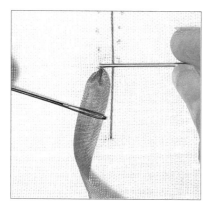

2. Anchor the ribbon at point A, hold it flat with the eye of a second needle, then take the ribbon back through the fabric close to where it came up.

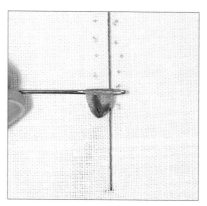

3. Pull the ribbon through from the back of the work until it is a fraction taller than the width of the ribbon.

4. Thread a needle with two strands of different shades of blue thread, then bring the needle up through the centre of the loop.

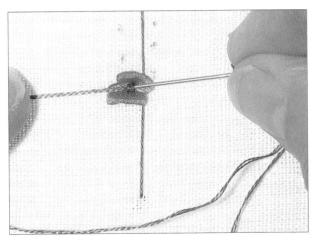

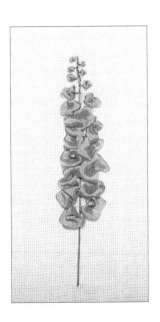

6. Continue up the stem, working florets B, C, D, etc., on either side of the stem, gradually making each straight-stitch loop smaller, and working tiny straight stitches for the last few buds. Work a one-loop French knot in the centre of the smaller florets.

Note: Normally, I would work most or all the straight-stitch loops up the length of the stem before sewing the French knots in the middle of each floret.

5. Work a two-loop French knot (see page 28), then take the needle back down through the centre of the stitch and pull it tight to flatten the loop and complete the floret.

Polyanthus and daffodils

See page 63 for details about making the basket, and page 79 for details about embroidering the flowers.

Ribbon Stitch

This stitch is unique to ribbon embroidery, as the needle is taken through both the ribbon and the fabric for each stitch. The needle can be passed through the ribbon at any point across its width to create a wide range of curled shapes. Varying the tension applied to each stitch can produce realistic three-dimensional flowers.

Wild rose

The curved up outer edges of these petals are worked with ribbon stitches where the needle is taken down through the middle of the ribbon. For this example, I used 7mm pink (08) ribbon, toning thread to anchor the ribbon and a yellow thread for the stamens.

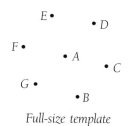

E •   • D

F •

      • A

          • C

G •

   • B

Full-size template

Tip

As a general rule when rolling ribbon over a second needle, use the same size needle as the one used to stitch the ribbon.

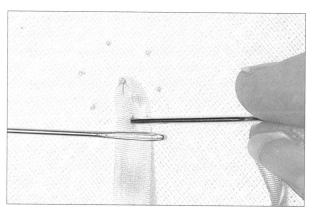

1. Anchor the end of the ribbon at point A. Hold the ribbon flat with a second needle over point B, then take the threaded needle and ribbon down through the middle of the ribbon.

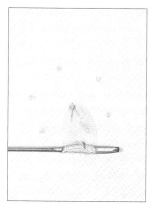

2. Leaving the second needle in the loop, pull the ribbon tight.

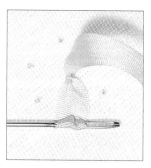

3. Still leaving the second needle in place, bring the ribbon back up at point A to start the second petal.

4. Continue working round the template, until all the petals are finished.

5. Use two strands of the yellow thread to create some twisted stamens (see page 20), and one strand to surround these with one-loop French knots.

Iris

This is a particularly attractive flower when worked in two colours. You can use many combinations of colour, but here I chose to use 7mm, cream (156) and deep yellow (15) ribbon.

Although each petal is a ribbon stitch, the different shapes are made by taking the needle down through the ribbon at different points across its width.

B •   • C

A
○

E •

• D   F
       •

Full-size template

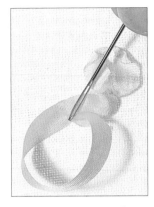

1. Anchor the cream ribbon at point A, flatten it with a second needle, then, holding the eye of that needle at an angle close to the right-hand edge of the ribbon, take the ribbon down through the right-hand edge of the ribbon at point B.

2. Keeping the eye end of the needle at an angle, gently pull the ribbon tight to form a cone-shaped roll at the top of the stitch.

3. Bring the ribbon back up through point A, then repeat steps 1 and 2, but take the ribbon down through the left-hand edge of the ribbon at point C with the eye of the second needle placed as shown. Fasten off the ribbon.

4. Anchor the deep yellow ribbon at point A, then, using a second needle as before, work a left-hand ribbon stitch through point D on the lower edge.

5. Work a right-hand ribbon stitch taking the needle down at point E (on the top edge) for the right-hand petal.

6. Bring the needle up through at point A and work a looser centre ribbon stitch taking the needle down at point F.

The finished flower shown full size.

25

Canterbury bell

The bell-shape of this flower is achieved by working the base petals with reverse centre ribbon stitches, then working a left, right and centre ribbon stitch on top. I worked this flower with 7mm, mid blue (126) ribbon and toning embroidery thread.

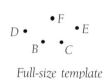

Full-size template

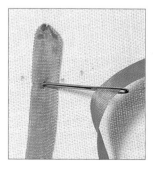

1. Anchor the ribbon at point A, flatten the ribbon and use the point of the needle to mark the position of point B in the middle of the ribbon.

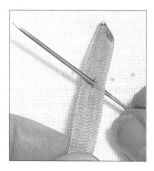

2. Lift the ribbon off the fabric and bring the needle up through the mark from the underside.

3. Pull the ribbon through the hole to form a loop, then place the eye of a second needle in the loop.

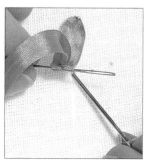

4. Tighten the loop against the second needle to form a shallow roll then take the ribbon down at point B.

5. Keeping the needle in the loop, bring the ribbon back up through point A. Pull the ribbon until the second needle is flat on the fabric, then remove the second needle.

6. Repeat steps 1–5 for another reverse centre stitch through point C, then work the third petal with a normal left-hand ribbon stitch, through point D.

7. Now work the fourth petal with a right-hand ribbon stitch through point E as shown.

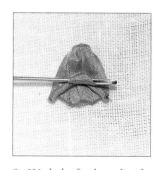

8. Work the final petal with a centre ribbon stitch through point F. When pulling the ribbon through to the back, take care not to distort the other petals.

9. Finally, use one strand of yellow thread to make a few one-loop French knots (see page 28) for the stamens.

Martagon lily (Turk's cap lily)

This flower has a delightful shape and, to create the petals, the ribbon is given a single twist before working the ribbon stitch. I used a 7mm dusky red (114) ribbon for this example, but a smaller, more delicate flower can be created with 4mm or 2mm ribbons.

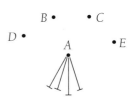

Full-size template

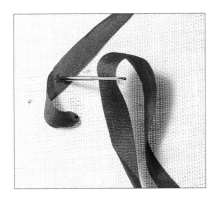

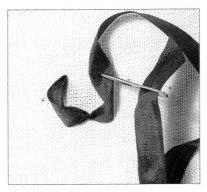

1. Anchor the ribbon at point A, twist the ribbon once, then take the needle through the ribbon at point B to create a centre ribbon stitch.

2. Bring the needle back up at point A and repeat step 1 to work a centre ribbon stitch at point C.

3. Work the other two petals at points D and E, then use the green thread to work four straight-stitch stamens. Use two strands of red thread to work a tiny straight stitch across the end of each stamen.

Rudbeckia

Forming the petals for this interesting flower involves using yet another variation of the ribbon stitch. Here, the 7mm deep gold (54) ribbon is folded along its length before the stitches are worked. The seed head is worked with French knots made with one strand from each of two shades of brown thread.

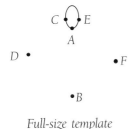

Full-size template

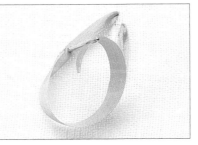

1. Anchor the ribbon at point A, lay the ribbon flat over point B, then fold the left-hand edge of the ribbon to the centre of the ribbon and work a centre ribbon stitch through B.

2. Repeat step 1 for a second petal worked between points C and D, and a third petal between points E and F. Now work a series of different length petals in between. Complete the flower by filling the oval shape with a series of two-loop French knots worked with the brown threads.

French knots

French knots instantly add texture and a new dimension to any design.
They can be made in different sizes and used for lots of flowers. One
large knot can represent a single bloom whereas a cluster of smaller ones
can be used for a large flower head. Small knots are particularly useful for
distant flowers, and a series of different sizes of knots are ideal for
creating perspective in a design.

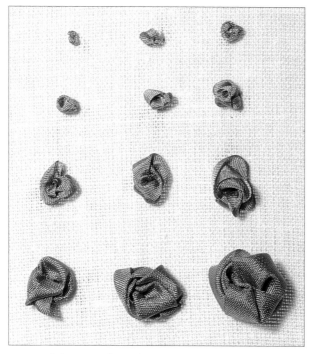

*French knots can be made in a multitude of different sizes
dependent on the width of the ribbon and the number of loops
wrapped round the needle and the tension applied to the stitch.
The knots can also be controlled with a second needle to create
even more shapes. The knots shown here are made with 2, 4, 7
and 13mm ribbon (top to bottom) and worked with 1, 2 and 3
loops round the needle (left to right).*

Tip

 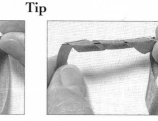

*Twist the ribbon as you
wind it round the needle.*

*Do not wind the ribbon
flat round the needle – it
will slide inside itself and
lose its bulk.*

Tip

*As a general rule, when using shades of the same
colour, the lightest shade indicates that the flower is
larger and more open; for relatively smaller, less open
flowers, deeper tones are used.*

*On the other hand, more distant (smaller) flowers are
made with paler shades of colour than the same (larger)
flower in the foreground.*

*This group of one-, two- and three-loop French knots
are all worked with 4mm ribbon. Tension
determines the size of each knot.*

Spray of roses

French knots are perfect for creating roses. This design is worked in one-, two- and three-loop French knots with three shades of pink 7mm ribbon: pink (08), mid pink (24) and bright pink (25). The leaves are worked with 7mm, deep green (21) ribbon over green thread stems.

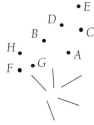

Full-size template

1. Anchor a length of pink ribbon at point A, then wrap three loops round the needle.

2. Place the tip of the needle through the fabric close to point A.

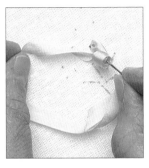

3. Gently pull the left-hand part of the ribbon until the knot is the right size . . .

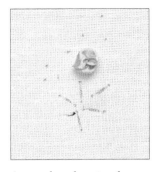

4. . . . then, keeping the ribbon under tension with your finger, pull the threaded needle through to the back of the fabric.

5. Repeat steps 1–4 at point B, then fasten off.

6. Anchor the mid pink ribbon at point C, work a two-loop knot there and at point D, then fasten off.

7. Anchor the bright pink ribbon at point E and work a one-loop knot for the smallest flower.

8. Gently pull the ribbon until the top knot is the right size, then fasten off.

9. Use mid pink ribbon to work two one-loop knots at points F and G, and bright pink ribbon for a smaller, one-loop knot at point H.

10. Finish the embroidery with straight stitch stems and a spray of ribbon stitch leaves.

Bells of Ireland

This tall majestic flower, similar in shape to the delphinium on page 22, comes in various shades of green. Each trumpet-shaped floret is worked by holding the ribbon flat over the eye end of a second needle as it is gently pulled through the fabric. I used green coton à broder for the stem, 7mm, moss green (20) ribbon for the florets, and white embroidery thread for the stamens. Here, I have worked one complete floret, but, normally, I would work all the bells before working the centres. The photographs for steps 2–4 are larger than life to show more detail.

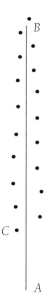

Full-size template

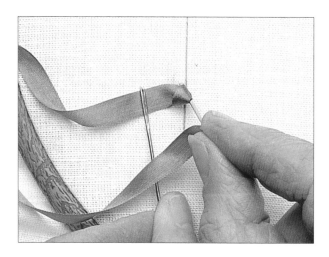

1. Use green coton à broder to make a straight stitch stem from point A to B as shown on page 22. Anchor the ribbon at point C, wind a single loop round the needle, then hold the ribbon flat with a second needle.

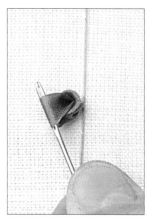

2. Keeping the ribbon flat against the second needle, gently pull the ribbon through the fabric . . .

3. . . . until the knot is the right size.

4. Use two strands of white thread to work a two-loop French knot in the centre of the floret.

5. Working alternately, from side to side up the stem, repeat steps 1–4, gradually reducing the size of each floret.

30

Primula candelabra

These flowers also have trumpet-shaped florets, but a slightly different technique is used to create the shape. Each group of flowers sit in a flat layer round the stem. These flowers can be found in a wide range of colours: from endless shades of cream to yellow, peach and reds. For this example, I used a 4mm, soft orange (16) ribbon. Again, the stem is green coton à broder.

Full-size template

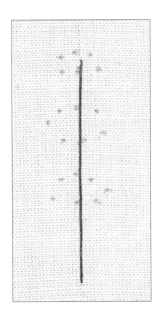

1. Work a straight stitch stem from points A–B as shown on page 22.

2. Bring the needle and ribbon up at point C, work a one-loop French knot round the needle, then take the needle down through the flat ribbon at point D.

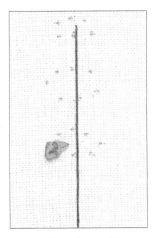

3. Gently pull the ribbon through to the back of the fabric to tighten the knot and form a trumpet shape.

4. Bring the needle up at point E and make another one-loop French knot at point F. Work the flowers round the stem making the knots at the back a little smaller than those at the front.

5. Use a single strand of thread to tone with the stem and work small straight stitches to connect each flower to the same point on the stem.

6. Repeat steps 2–5 for the other florets, making each layer slightly smaller.

Honeysuckle

This is a lovely plant that climbs and meanders everywhere. It has the most unusual flowers, with petals that twist to form irregular shapes. No two flowers are the same. I have included the template I used for this example, which I worked with 2mm, soft yellow (14) ribbon. When you have worked this first flower, design others with different shapes and sizes of petals. For clarity, all the photographs, except the finished flower, are reproduced larger than life.

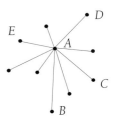

Full-size template

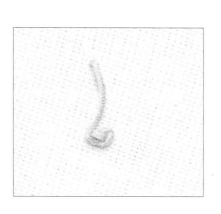

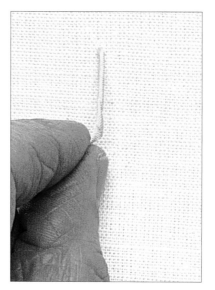

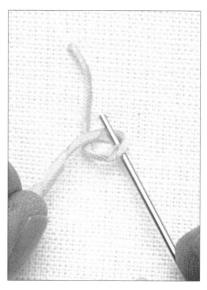

1. Bring the ribbon up through point A (the centre of the flower), then twist the ribbon several times.

2. Hold the twisted ribbon between finger and thumb, then slide them down the ribbon to tighten the twists into a tubular shape.

3. Keeping the ribbon twisted, work a one-loop French knot round the needle, then take the needle down at point B.

4. As the knot is pulled tight, the ribbon will distort to create the characteristic, uneven shape of the honeysuckle petal.

5. Work similar knots between point A and C, D and E to create the shape of the flower head, then continue working round the flower filling in the gaps – vary the number of twists and the length of each petal.

Blossom

To create the lovely mixture of colours found in summer blossom, I like to work with two ribbons and harmonious colours in the needle to make each French knot. The twists in the ribbons create the beautiful colours that can be seen in the lovely eye-catching blossom. For this example, I combined 4mm, white (03) and pink (08) ribbon to create a delightful range of subtle shades, but there are many other colour combinations that could be used.

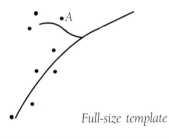

Full-size template

1. Use one strand each of two tones of brown embroidery thread to work straight stitches for the stem. Couch the stems to the curve on the pattern with one strand of toning thread.

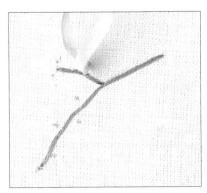

2. Knot lengths of the pink and white ribbon together, thread them into a size 18 needle, then, keeping both ribbons even, bring the needle and ribbons up through point A.

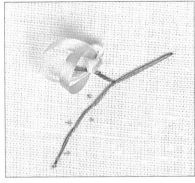

3. Work a one-loop French knot with both ribbons, taking care to pull both ribbons through evenly.

4. Keep pulling the ribbon until the knot is the required size.

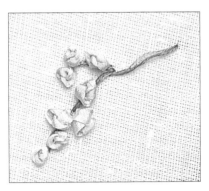

5. Working down the stem, repeat steps 3 and 4 to make French knots at all the other points on the template. Make each knot a slightly different size.

Gathering

Making flowers with a gathered ribbon is a very versatile technique, particularly when the flowers are worked life size. On these and the following few pages I show you a range of gathering methods that can be used to create many different flowers. Try working these particular flowers, and you will soon learn that by simply altering the length of the gathered ribbon many other types of flowers can be created.

> ## Tip
> *Use one strand of ribbon-coloured embroidery thread to gather the ribbon and one of fabric-coloured thread to anchor it. This makes threads easy to identify so you avoid accidentally cutting the gathering thread.*

Scabious

This lovely, light and delicate flower has a large, pincushion centre, surrounded by a frill of petals. For this example, I used a 7mm wide, delph blue (117) ribbon for the petals, one strand each of pale cream and pale green embroidery thread for the stamens, green coton à broder for the stem and 2mm deep green (21) ribbon for the leaves.

Full-size template

> ## Tip
> *Remember that the centres of different types of flower vary in size.*
> *You must also adjust the size of the flower centre to match the width of ribbon used.*

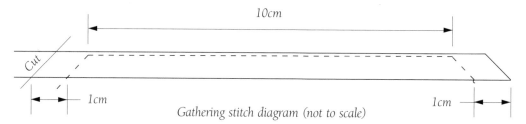

10cm

Cut

1cm

1cm

Gathering stitch diagram (not to scale)

1. Referring to the gathering stitch diagram above, carefully cut the ribbon to size. Knot the end of one strand of toning thread, bring the needle through the selvedge of one long side of the ribbon, 1cm from the end, then work a tiny stitch over this edge to anchor the knot (for clarity, I used a contrasting colour for these photographs).

2. Work a row of small running stitches across the ribbon parallel to the cut end of ribbon.

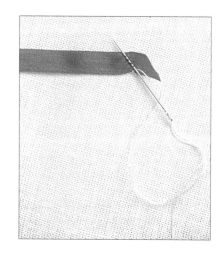

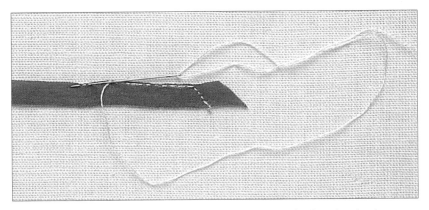

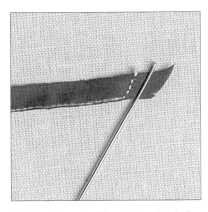

3. Work a 10cm row of small running stitches along the selvedge, then back across the ribbon at an angle of 45°.

4. Pass the end of the ribbon (with the thread knot) into the eye of a size 18 needle and position the needle parallel to the diagonal stitches.

Tip

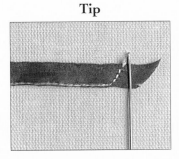

When anchoring the ribbon the angled stitch line must sit exactly in the thickness of the fabric. If in step 4 the needle is positioned as shown here, the diagonal row of running stitches will sit either side of the fabric and spoil the shape of the petal.

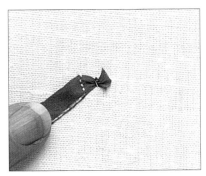

5. Holding the ribbon flat on the fabric, pull the needle and the unsewn end of ribbon through the fabric so the thread knot is just on the underside and the angled row of stitches is sitting in the thickness of the fabric.

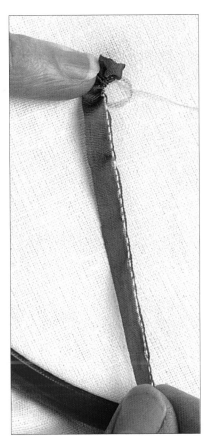

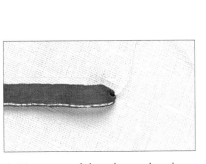

6. Use a second thread to anchor the ribbon behind where the frill is to be placed, then bring this thread up through the fabric close to where the ribbon comes through. (Any ribbon anchored across the centre of the flower will cause problems).

7. Draw the centre circle on the fabric, then gather a short length of the ribbon (close to where it comes up through the fabric) by gently pulling on the loose end of the gathering thread.

8. Use the anchor thread and small stab stitches to secure the gathered ribbon round the circle. Continue to gather and stitch until you have worked one third of the way round the circle.

9. Now, take the other end of the ribbon through to the back, next to the start point, then fasten off with the anchoring thread. Take care not to sew through the gathering thread.

10. Hold the ribbon down lightly with a finger and gently pull the gathering thread until the gathered edge sits round the circle.

11. Use the gathering thread to stab stitch the gathered edge round the circle, then fasten off.

12. Use one strand each of pale cream and green thread to work three, two-loop French knots in the centre, then surround these with one-loop knots. Work a straight stitch stem, then add a few 2mm, ribbon stitch leaves.

Poppy

The beauty of this life-size field poppy is its basic simplicity. I used a 13mm, red (02) ribbon, gathered in a particular way to suggest the shape of the petals. I also used 7mm moss green (20) ribbon, and green and black thread for the flower centre.

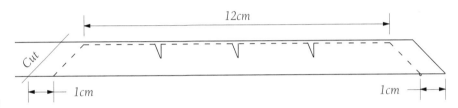

Gathering stitch diagram (not to scale)

Full-size template

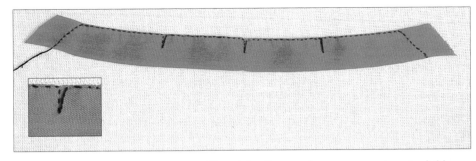

1. Referring to steps 1–3 on pages 34–35, and the diagram above, prepare a length of ribbon. As you stitch along the selvedge, work three equally spaced vertical stitches down to the middle of the ribbon, then tiny running stitches back to the selvedge.

2. Anchor the ribbon on the circle (see page 35, steps 4–6) then start to gather it up to the first vertical stitch; notice how the ribbon is drawn down to the centre. Stab stitch the gathered selvedge to the circle.

3. Gather and stab stitch the next two sections. Anchor the other end of the ribbon (see page 36, step 9), gather and stab stitch the last section to the circle and fasten off.

4. If the two ends of the ribbon do not sit neatly and leave a gap, use the gathering thread to catch the selvedge at each side of the gap, then work a single stitch to draw the sides together. Take the thread down through the fabric close to the anchored edge, but do not pull the thread too tight. Fasten off.

5. Use the moss green ribbon to work a straight stitch in the flower centre. Use one strand of the green thread to criss-cross the green ribbon. Use two strands of black thread to work a cluster of one-loop French knots round the flower centre.

Anemone

This flower has a similar but more positive shape than the poppy. I used a 13mm, deep pink (128) ribbon and a different method of gathering to create this particular effect. I also used green thread for a stem, black and white thread to work the detail in the flower centre and 2mm deep green (21) ribbon to work a few ribbon stitch leaves.

Full-size pattern

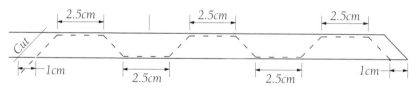

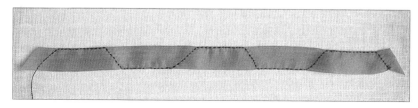

Gathering stitch diagram (not to scale)

1. Anchor the gathering thread to the selvedge (see page 34) then, referring to the diagram above, work the gathering stitches, crossing the ribbon at 45°.

2. Anchor the knot end of the ribbon on the circle and bring the thread to the front. Gather the first section and stab stitch this gathered selvedge round the circle.

3. Fold the ribbon up, along the first diagonal row of gathering stitches, to bring the next straight gathered section down to the edge of the circle.

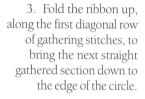

4. Keeping the fold in place with your finger, continue to gather and stab stitch each of the next three petals round the circle. Before gathering the last section, anchor the end of the ribbon just behind and slightly overlapping the start of the first petal.

5. Finish gathering and anchor off the thread on the back of the fabric.

6. Use two strands of black thread to work a cluster of two-loop French knots in the centre, then surround these with one-loop knots. Use one strand of white thread to encircle the black centre with one-loop knots.

38

Pansy

This is one of the most colourful of all flowers. It is worked with two lengths of ribbon, in one or two colours. Here, I used 13mm, pale mauve (178) ribbon for both lengths, then, after completing the flower I shaded the petals with silk paint (see page 69). I then used 4mm deep yellow (15) ribbon and a short straight stitch to fill the flower centre, coton à broder and a straight stitch for a stem, and 7mm deep moss green (72) ribbon for three centre ribbon stitch leaves.

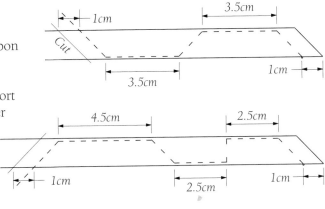

Full-size template

Gathering stitch diagrams (not to scale)

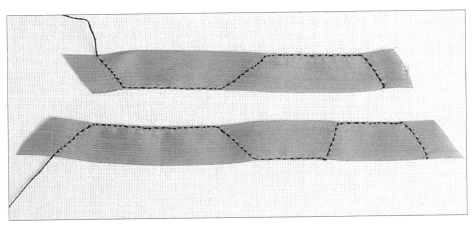

1. Referring to the instructions on pages 34–35, work the gathering stitches to the measurements shown in the diagram above.

2. Anchor the short length of ribbon at point A, gather and fold the ribbon as for the anemone on page 38 (steps 2–3) then stab stitch the gathered edge round to point B. Fasten off.

3. Anchor the long ribbon at point C, then repeat step 2, gathering, folding and stitching the first two sections round the top half of the circle to point D.

4. Fold the ribbon along the diagonal at point D, anchor the loose end of the ribbon at point C, in front of and slightly overlapping the start of the frill.

5. Gather the last length round the lower edge of the circle, stab stitch in place, then fasten off.

The finished pansy

39

Aquilegia

This is a delicately frilled flower that hangs downward and sits like a bonnet; hence, its common name of Granny's bonnet. The gathering is similar to that for the poppy, but the straight stitches are set at an angle, rather than vertical, to distort the frill and petals even more. I used a 13mm, cream (156) ribbon, then, when the petals were finished, I lightly painted the ribbon to shade them. I then used 4mm pale mauve (178) ribbon to work five straight stitch top petals and yellow thread for the twisted stamens.

Full-size template

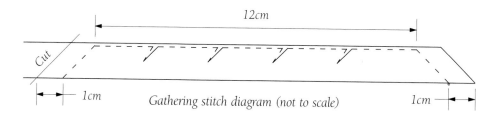

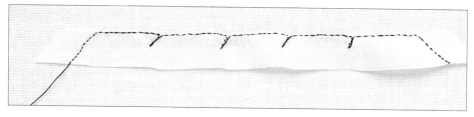

1. Anchor the gathering thread (see page 35), then sew the gathering stitches as shown, making four long stitches, similar to those for the poppy on page 37, but at an angle.

2. Anchor the knot end of the ribbon at point A.

3. Gather, then stab stitch the selvedge round the oval end to point B.

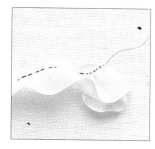

4. Turn the ribbon so that the gathered edge is at the top of the ribbon and stab stitch across the top of the oval to point C.

Tip
When working round an oval shape, gathering the ribbon more at the narrow ends than at the flatter sides will allow the frill to sit neatly.

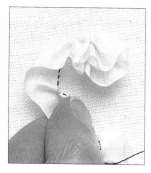

5. Fold the ribbon again, gather the next section of the ribbon and stab stitch round the oval to point D.

6. Anchor the end of the ribbon close to the start point A, gather the last length of the ribbon and stab stitch in place.

The finished flower. I added a straight stitch stem.

Sweet pea

This flower is a true favourite of mine, and just a little paint will enable you to reproduce their exciting range of colours. Each flower is worked with two lengths of ribbon. This life-size flower is made from 13mm, soft blue (125) ribbon which I painted before starting to embroider the flower.

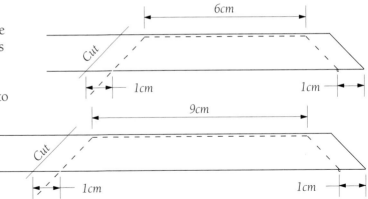

Gathering stitch diagrams (not to scale)

Full-size pattern. You only need to transfer the straight line on to the fabric.

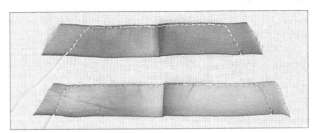

1. Prepare two lengths of ribbon as shown, fold them in half, then iron a crease across the middle of each piece.

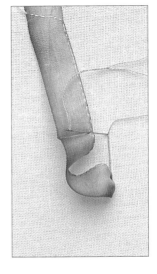

2. Anchor the knot end of the long ribbon at point A, just to the left of the line, and bring the thread up at point B. Take the thread down through the selvedge of the ribbon at the crease (avoiding the gathering stitches) and through the fabric at point B.

3. Bring the thread up at point A, then gather the ribbon up to the crease to form a shallow vertical curve. Make the gathers slightly tighter at the top. Stab stitch the gathered edge up the curve.

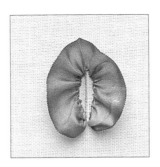

4. Anchor the other end of the ribbon at point C, just to the right of the line, gather and stitch the ribbon along the other curve, then fasten off.

5. Repeat steps 2–4 with the short ribbon, but, this time, stab stitch the gathered edge along the outer edge so that this petal stands up.

The finished sweet pea. I added a straight stitch stem and two straight stitch leaves worked with 2mm ribbon.

Lazy daisy stitch

This traditional stitch, also known as detached chain stitch, is a useful, easy stitch to work. It is particularly useful for embroidering irises, but it can also be used for other types of flowers.

Irises

The iris may be worked either as a closed or an open flower. The size of each flower can be changed by using different width ribbons (see page 8) and altering the length of stitch. Here, I show you how to work a closed flower first, then an open one. I used 4mm, pale mauve (178) ribbon for the top petals and 4mm, mid mauve (179) for the lower petals or fall.

Closed irises

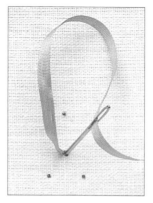

1. Anchor the end of the pale mauve ribbon just to one side of point A, then take it down just on the other side.

2. Pull the ribbon through the fabric to form a loop that just fits comfortably around the point B.

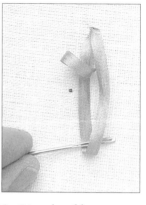

3. Bring the ribbon up at point B and through the loop. Hold the ribbon flat with a second needle, then take it over the loop and down at point B.

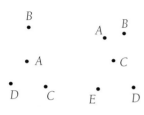

Full-size templates for a closed iris (left) and an open flower (right).

4. Keep the ribbon flat and under tension with the second needle, then pull the ribbon through the fabric to make a flat stitch to anchor the first loop. Fasten off.

5. Anchor the mid mauve ribbon at point C, then, using the eye of the needle, slide the ribbon behind the top petals. Take the ribbon down through point D, pull it through the fabric to form a soft loop, then fasten off.

The finished closed iris.

Open irises

1. Anchor the pale mauve ribbon at point A, take it down at point B and pull it through the fabric to form a loop that just fits comfortably around point C. Now repeat steps 3 and 4 (of the Closed iris), but work the anchoring loop at point C.

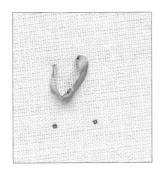

2. Anchor the mid mauve ribbon at point D, then use the eye end of the needle to pass the ribbon through the small anchoring loop at point C.

3. Take the ribbon down through the fabric at point E, pull it through the fabric to form a soft loop, then fasten off.

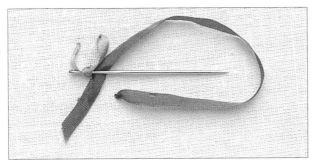

The finished open iris

Group of irises

This little group of irises are all worked in lazy daisy stitch using 4 and 7mm ribbon. See page 79 for details about embroidering this design.

Tip

When embroidering an iris with 7mm ribbon, take the ribbon through the fabric behind the petals to prevent too much bulk at the base of the loop.

Bleeding heart

This interesting and delicate flower is worked with a modified lazy daisy stitch. I used a 4mm, dusky red (114) ribbon for the top petals and pink (08) for the lower ones. I used two strands of spice coloured thread to work the stem and side shoots.

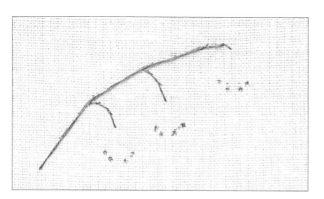

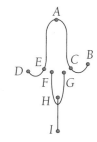

Full-size template and enlarged detail of flower template.

1. Use a spice coloured thread to work a single straight stitch stem, couch it along the curve, then work the side shoots.

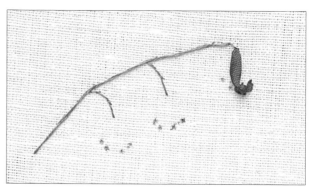

2. Anchor the dusky red ribbon at point A and take it down at point B to leave a loop. Bring the ribbon up at point C, then, controlling it over a second needle, take the ribbon over the first loop and back down again at point C. Pull the ribbon through the fabric to make a flat stitch to anchor the first loop.

3. Repeat step 2, working a reverse-angle petal through points A, D and E, then fasten off.

4. Anchor the pink ribbon at point F, make a loop round point H and take the ribbon back at point G. Bring the ribbon up at point H, through the loop and back down again at point I. Pull this stitch tight then fasten off.

The finished flower.

44

Rosebud

Tiny rosebuds are so attractive and useful. They are easy to work with a lazy daisy stitch. I would normally use 2 or 4mm ribbon, but I used a 7mm, mid pink (24) ribbon for this demonstration to show how good it can look at a larger size.

Anchor the ribbon at point A, make a loop that just encloses point B, then take the ribbon down again at point A. Bring the ribbon up at point B and through the loop. Controlling the ribbon over a second needle, set at an angle as shown, and take it down at point C. Pull the ribbon to form a small stitch to anchor the first loop, then fasten off.

B •• C

Full-size template • A

The finished flower.

Broom, bluebells and red-hot pokers

This little cameo is embroidered with variations of lazy daisy stitch worked with 2mm ribbon. I shaded white ribbon with blue silk paint (see page 64) before working the bluebells, and painted the red hot pokers, after working them, with tones of yellow, orange and red.

You will need

Fabric
15 x 20cm piece of cotton evenweave

2mm ribbons
2m of deep yellow (15)
66cm of deep green (21)
66cm of soft green (33)
1.5m of white (03)

Threads
A variety of toning embroidery threads

Silk paints
Red, blue and yellow

Enlarge this diagram to 200% for a full-size pattern

Leaves

Every plant has its own distinctive leaves. The colour of the leaf, its size in relation to that of the flower, and how it is connected to the plant – from the stem or direct from the ground – are all equally important factors to consider. I have worked a variety of leaves opposite to illustrate.

1. This leaf is a single centre-ribbon stitch.

2. This is a similar, but much larger, version of leaf 1. It consists of a left- and right-ribbon stitch worked together in a similar manner to the top half of the iris on page 25.

3. This leaf is worked with three centre-ribbon stitches fanning out from the base.

4. This leaf also consists of three ribbon stitches, but it has straight stitches worked with six strands of toning embroidery thread that are placed to mirror the ribbon stitches.

5. These leaves are straight stitches, each worked from the centre out to the tip, with the ribbon controlled over a second needle (see page 18).

6. Although this is not strictly a leaf, moss can be very useful in a garden design. This example is worked in thread with one- and two-loop French knots.

7. Another leaf worked with ribbon stitches.

8. A straight-stitch leaf where the ribbon is twisted and pulled tight to reflect its stiffness.

9. A similar shape to example 8, but, here, each leaf is worked with a ribbon stitch.

10. Another variation of straight-stitch leaves.

11. I associate this special shape with a fern, and create it with a gathered ribbon stitch. To work this example, start by working a 4cm length of gathering stitches through the centre of a long length of 7mm ribbon. Mark two dots on the fabric, 3cm apart, to indicate the length of the leaf, then anchor the knot end of the gathering at the stem end of the leaf. Work a ribbon stitch at the other end, leaving the gathering thread on the front of the fabric. Pull this thread to create the leaf shapes, then use it to secure the ribbon. Use the same thread to stitch along the gathered line to create a vein and to hold the leaf down on the fabric.

12. These ivy leaves are small versions of example 3.

13. This holly leaf is worked in a similar manner to leaf 11, but the ribbon is not gathered. Start by marking two dots for the length of the leaf, 2cm apart, on the fabric. Anchor the ribbon at the stem end, hold the ribbon flat, put the needle into the ribbon 3cm away from the anchored end, then pass the needle through the second dot to leave a loop. Anchor this end of the ribbon, then work a row of back stitches along the centre of the ribbon, puckering it to flatten the loop along its length. Work a tiny lazy daisy stitch to pull out each fold and create the prickles.

14. These mistletoe leaves are all straight stitches.

15. I know that a fir cone is not a leaf, but it does have an interesting shape, and it is a must with holly and mistletoe. It is somewhat difficult to embroider, so practise first. Lightly draw the cone shape on to the fabric, anchor the ribbon at point A, then work modified lazy daisy stitches, through points B, C, D, E, F, etc., as shown below, keeping a fairly loose tension.

 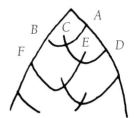

Full-size template.   *Enlargement to show stitch detail.*

16. This cow parsley comprises a series of straight stitches worked with two strands of thread for the main stem and one for all the others.

17. Grasses are always useful. In this example, the blades of grass are all straight stitches worked with different types and colours of threads.

Laburnum arches

This design of irises and foxgloves, with aubretia edging the path under a laburnum archway, uses four basic stitches. The three-dimensional effect is created by using various ribbon widths and shades of colour. The irises in the foreground, for example, are worked in 7mm ribbon, while those in the middle distance are worked in 4mm and those in the background are worked in 2mm ribbon. Three different colours are used to create light and shade among the laburnums. I have listed the lengths and colours of the ribbons used for this embroidery, but there are many other colours you could use to great effect.

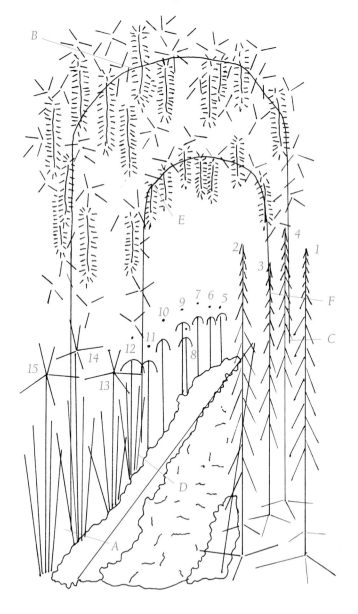

Enlarge this diagram to 150% for a full-size template

You will need

Fabric
30 x 40cm piece of medium weight calico
10cm square of textured spiced-colour fabric (cotton/muslin)

Ribbons for the laburnum
100cm, 2mm cream (156)
150cm, 2mm khaki (56)
700cm, 2mm deep yellow (15)
200cm, 4mm moss green (20)
150cm, 4mm bright green (60)
100cm, 4mm deep moss green (72)

Ribbons for the foxgloves
66cm, 4mm just blue (100)
100cm, 4mm pale mauve (178)
50cm, 4mm mid mauve (179)
166cm, 7mm purple (177)
100cm, 7mm mid mauve (179)
100cm, 7mm pale mauve (178)
66cm, 7mm deep green (21)
66cm, 4mm deep moss green (72)

Ribbons for the irises
33cm, 2mm mid blue (126)
33cm, 2mm cream (156)
33cm, 2mm deep yellow (15)
33cm, 4mm deep blue (46)
33cm, 4mm soft yellow (14)
66cm, 7mm pale blue (44)
66cm, 7mm delph blue (117)
150cm, 4mm soft green (33)
66cm, 2mm soft green (33)

Ribbons for the aubretia
66cm, 2mm dusky pink (163)
66cm, 2mm pale mauve (178)
133cm, 4mm deep pink (128)
133cm, 4mm purple (177)
33cm, 4mm just blue (100)
33cm, 4mm white (03)
33cm, 7mm deep green (21)
33cm, 7mm moss green (20)

Threads

Moss green cotton perle for the arch Mid green coton à broder for the iris and moss green for the foxgloves. Toning stranded embroidery threads (including sand, soft brown and donkey for the arch).

Arch

1. Tack round the outside edge of the design, then transfer the shape of the arches and path on to the fabric.

2. Add two strands each of khaki, soft brown and donkey coloured thread to a length of moss green perle. Take the ends of this group of threads through to the back of the fabric at point A, secure with a toning thread and use this thread to couch the arch in place to point B. Take half the stranded threads to the back and fasten off. Couch the remaining threads to point C and fasten off. Repeat for second arch at D, E and F.

Laburnum

1. Transfer the laburnum flowers to the fabric. Embroider each flower with a tiny straight stitch worked in 2mm ribbon. Most of these flowers are deep yellow, some are highlighted with cream, and those in shadow are worked with khaki ribbon.

2. Use one strand of pale green embroidery thread to work a straight stitch through the centre and another, tiny one to connect each flower to its stem.

3. Use ribbon stitch and 4mm moss green ribbon to create most of the leaves. Use bright green for highlighted leaves and deep moss for those in shadow.

Path

1. Roll the small piece of spice-coloured fabric into a tight ball and press creases in it with a hot iron.

2. Open out the creased fabric, cut out the shape of the path and tack this on to the background fabric.

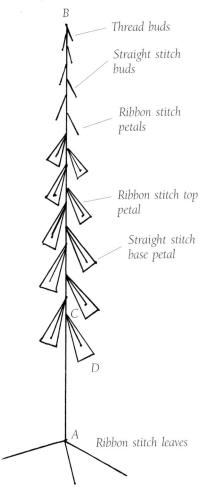

Template for basic foxglove

Labels on template:
- B
- Thread buds
- Straight stitch buds
- Ribbon stitch petals
- Ribbon stitch top petal
- Straight stitch base petal
- C
- D
- A
- Ribbon stitch leaves

Colour code for foxgloves

Flower 1 7mm purple base petals and pale mauve top petals. 4mm deep green leaves.

Flower 2 7mm purple base petals and mid mauve top petals. 4mm deep green leaves.

Flower 3 4mm purple base petals, pale mauve top petals and deep moss leaves.

Flower 4 4mm pale mauve base petals, just blue top petals and deep moss leaves.

Foxgloves

1. Mark the foxgloves 1–4 on the fabric. Referring to the template for the basic foxgloves (left), use moss green coton à broder to work straight stitch stems between points A and B (see page 22).

2. Now, referring to the colour code, anchor the ribbon at point C, then using a second needle to control the ribbon, work a straight stitch base petal to point D (see page 18). Continue working up the stem, alternating the stitches from side to side, making each new stitch a little smaller than the previous one. Stop 2.5–3cm from the top and fasten off.

3. Anchor the second colour at point C, lay the ribbon over the first stitch and place the needle in the ribbon at point D, and work a centre ribbon stitch (see page 24) into the centre of the base petal. Continue up the stem working centre ribbon stitches over all the existing straight stitch base petals. Then, use the same colour to work the next two flowers with just ribbon stitches.

4. Embroider the buds with straight stitches worked from the tip to the stem, making each bud a little smaller as you work up the stem. Fasten off the ribbon 0.5–1cm from the top.

5. Release the green stem thread, pull it through to the back to re-tension the stem, then re-thread the needle. Keeping the thread taut bring it up to the front just below the top of the stem. Work a straight stitch into the top of the stem to form a tiny closed bud, add more buds as required, and finish at the opposite side of the top ribbon bud.

6. Bring the needle up through the first bud and take it down through the stem (it must not cross over the stem) to form a calyx and so attach it to the stem. Work downwards, connecting each bud and flower to the stem, then fasten off behind the lowest flower.

7. Work the leaves in ribbon stitch.

Irises

1. Mark position of flowers 5–12 on the fabric, then, referring to the colour code and the instructions on page 42, work these as closed irises.

2. Work straight stitch stems: use one strand of green cotton thread on flowers 5–9 and coton à broder for flowers 10, 11, and 12.

3. Use green coton à broder to work the straight stitch leaves for flowers 5–9 and 2mm soft green ribbon for flowers 10–12.

4. Mark the positions of the open irises (flowers 13, 14 and 15) on the fabric, then referring to the colour code, embroider these as shown on page 25.

5. Use 2mm deep yellow ribbon to work a small straight stitch from the centre of the lower middle petal of flower 13 and fasten off. Repeat for flowers 14 and 15.

6. Use coton à broder to work a straight stitch stem on each flower.

7. Use 4mm ribbon to work the straight stitch leaves on each flower.

Colour code for irises

Flowers 5, 6 and 9 2mm mid blue ribbon petals and green coton à broder leaves.

Flowers 7 and 8 2mm cream ribbon petals and green coton à broder leaves.

Flowers 10 and 12 4mm soft yellow ribbon petals and 2mm soft green ribbon leaves.

Flower 11 4mm deep blue ribbon petals and 2mm soft green ribbon leaves.

Flowers 13, 14 and 15 7mm pale blue and delph blue petals and 4mm soft green ribbon leaves.

Aubretia

1. Cut a 17cm length of 7mm deep green ribbon and a 10cm length of 7mm moss green ribbon for the background.

2. Thread a length of 2mm dusky pink ribbon into a size 24 chenille needle and knot one end. Tuck one end of the deep green ribbon under foxglove 2, at the top of the path, and bring the needle up through the green ribbon.

3. Work a one-loop French knot to secure the ribbon, then work more knots at random, puckering the ribbon to make an uneven edge as you work along the path.

4. Change to 2mm pale mauve ribbon and work more one-loop French knots.

5. Keeping the deep green ribbon at the base, lay in the length of moss green ribbon, tucking the cut end under to make a wider border. Continue working one-loop French knots, first with the 4mm deep pink ribbon then the 4mm purple ribbon.

6. Fold the ends of the green ribbon under at the end of the path.

7. Use 4mm just blue and white ribbon to work French knots at random on the other side of the path.

Opposite
The finished embroidery
The spice-coloured path leads the eye under the arch, and the smaller flowers at the back of the picture create a feeling of distance.

Painting backgrounds

Lightly painting the background fabric is the most exciting way to transform any embroidery. You do not need a wide range of colours; I only ever work with the three primary colours (red, blue and yellow) from which I can mix any colour I need. Always start painting with pale colours, as it is much easier to build up tone gradually than to end up with a shade that is too deep. In this chapter I include two projects: the first, a country scene, has a structured background painted with fabric paints and gutta; the other, an arrangement of pansies, has a random pattern background worked with silk paints.

Tip

If you are not happy with your drawing skills, you can trace the design on to the fabric. Pin the paper pattern face down on the back of the fabric. Mount the fabric right side up in an embroidery frame. Hold the frame against a light source or window, then use a pencil to trace the design on to the fabric.

Country scene

This design shows how a painted background can enhance the three-dimensional effect of silk ribbon embroidery. It includes a number of painting techniques which you can use together or individually to create designs of your own.

For painting this project you will need red, blue and yellow fabric paints, a tile palette, silver gutta, a stiff brush and a round brush, and a piece of sponge. If you have never used fabric paints or gutta, practise on a spare piece of fabric before working the project.

Enlarge this diagram to 150% to make a full-size template

52

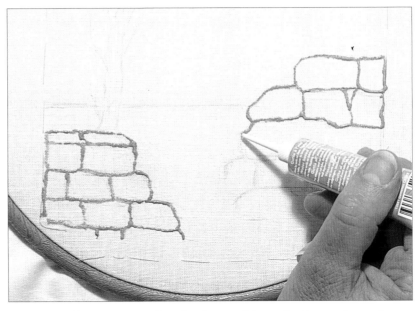

1. Tack guidelines round all four sides of the area to be painted, then use a pencil to draw in the shapes of the rocks, the horizon, and the outline of the tree trunk and branches.

2. Use the silver gutta to outline the shapes of the rocks. Ensure that each shape is totally enclosed without any breaks in the lines of gutta.

3. Use the three primary colours to mix a series of greys on a tile.

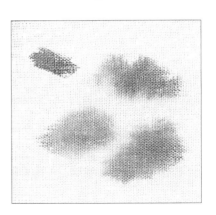

4. Wet a spare piece of fabric, then test your mixed colours.

5. Use a stiff brush to dampen each group of rocks with clean water – this helps spread the paint – then use a round brush to paint them. Combine different shades of grey to paint the rocks, so that you create patches of light and shade.

6. Thoroughly wet the sky area down to just above the horizon line; extend the wetting beyond the tacked border to allow paint to bleed out of the image area.

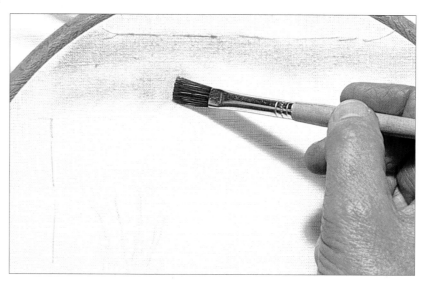

7. Mix blue fabric paint, with a touch of red, to create a very pale blue wash. Working quickly with long, horizontal strokes, brush in the sky from the top downwards.

8. Reduce the tone as you near the horizon by adding a little more water to the paint.

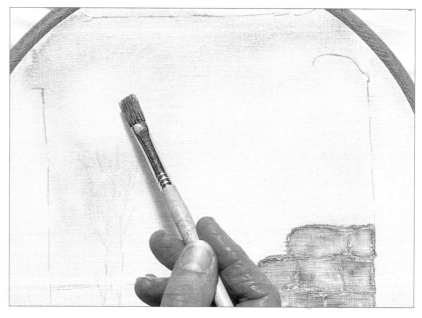

9. While the fabric is still wet, drop in a few spots of clean water; as the water spreads across the fabric it takes away some of the pigment to create clouds. Leave to dry.

Tip

A hairdryer is useful to either speed up drying time or to prevent paint seeping too far.

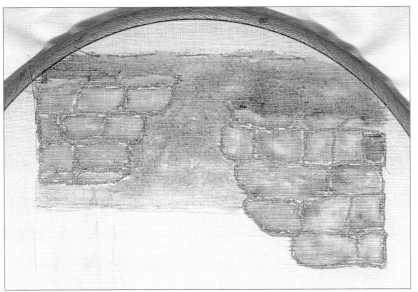

10. Mix a green from blue and yellow with a touch of red. Turn the picture upside down, lightly moisten the fabric, then paint the grassy area, diluting the colour as you reach the horizon line.

11. Moisten a sponge with clean water, then working very lightly, sponge in the green foliage of the left-hand tree.

12. When all the fabric is completely dry, remove it from the frame and press it with a medium hot iron to fix the dye. Mount the painted fabric back in the frame and embroider the flowers and foliage as described on the following pages.

Embroidering the design

1. Lay the green, dyed ribbon along the top of the horizon line, up to the left-hand side of the wall, then, using a toning thread, work a series of small straight stitches and fly stitches to pucker the ribbon. Keep the bottom edge straight and allow the top to undulate.

2. Arrange lengths of string for the tree trunk and unravel some for the narrower branches. Use a toning thread to couch these in position. Take the ends of each length of string through to the back and secure at the back with the couching thread. Use one strand of light green thread and tiny lazy daisy stitches to create leaves randomly on the tree.

3. Referring to page 49 and the pattern on page 52, embroider the foxgloves with ribbon and straight stitches. Flowers 1, 2 and 5 are worked with 7mm ribbon, 3, 4 and 6 with 4mm ribbon. Use dusky pink for the base petals for flowers 1–4 and deep pink for the top ones. Use pale mauve for the base petals of flowers 5 and 6, and dusky pink for the top petals.

4. Using two strands of green thread, couch the bluebell stems. Use the dyed blue ribbon and lazy daisy stitches to work the larger flower heads in a similar way to those of the bleeding heart on page 44. Use straight stitches for the buds at the top of each stem. Use the soft green ribbon and long, twisted, straight stitches for the leaves.

5. Use the moss green ribbon and straight stitches, similar to those used for the buttercup on page 18, to form the leaves of the primroses. Use the yellow ribbon to form five petals on each flower, working each from the tip to the centre and controlling the ribbon with a second needle. Use two strands of yellow thread to work a one-loop French knot in the centre of each flower. Form the buds with straight stitches. Use one strand of green thread to form the flower stems, and two strands to form the calyx of the buds.

6. Work the petals of the violets with deep mauve ribbon and ribbon stitch, then use one strand of yellow thread to make a French knot in the centre of each flower. Use one strand of green thread for the stems, then the soft green ribbon and straight stitch to form the leaves.

7. Couch two strands of pale brown thread for the ivy stems, then fan-shapes of three ribbon stitches for each leaf. Use two shades of green to create light and shade.

8. Using one strand of thread for each bird, work a fly stitch, couching the wings in curves. Use dark grey for the large birds and a paler shade for the smaller, more distant ones.

9. Use a variety of green threads to work clusters of one-loop French knots to form the patches of moss and a few grasses at the bottom right of the wall to finish the embroidery.

Opposite
The finished embroidery
The paler painted background gives a feeling of distance, which is enhanced by the strong detail in the foreground.

Pansies

For this design, the random pattern on the silk habotai background is created with silk paints. Painting patterns such as this is great fun; although you control the application of water and silk paints, you cannot really control the end result. Practise on spare pieces of silk and you will see just how easy it is. For this background, I mixed blue and magenta to form shades of blue and purple.

The pansies (see page 39) were worked, one at a time, in cream ribbon on a length of 7mm ribbon, kept very taut in a frame, then painted with silk paints. When they were completely dry, I cut the ribbon to leave 1cm tails on either side of each flower, then attached them to the painted silk background.

You will need
Fabric
25cm square of silk habotai
Ribbon
2.3m of 13mm cream (156)
Silk paints
Red, magenta, blue, yellow and clear gutta
Thread
Toning cream stranded thread

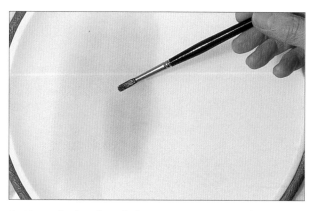

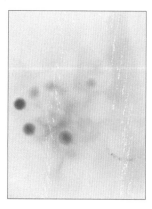

1. Use a flat brush and clean water to moisten the entire surface of the silk. Then, using a small round brush loaded with diluted colour, drop the first colour on to the wet fabric and note how it spreads out.

2. Quickly drop in a second colour.

3. Spatter spots of stronger colours over the still wet fabric.

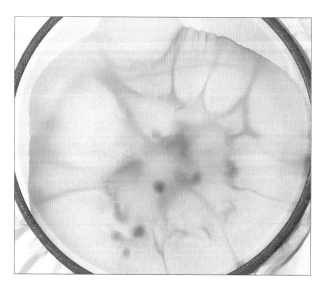

5. Add more spots of colour, then drop in spots of clean water. Notice how the clean water moves the pigments about.

4. Allow the colours to spread and merge together.

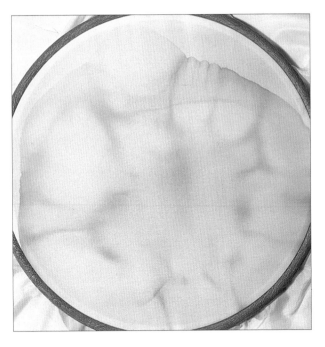

6. When you are happy with the result – stop the movement of the pigment by drying the fabric with a hairdryer. Remove the dry fabric from the frame and press it with a medium hot iron to fix the dye. Mount the painted fabric back in the frame.

7. Paint the flowers one at a time, leaving each colour to dry before applying the next. In the following instructions, the pansies are numbered 1–5, starting at top left.

Pansy 1 Mix yellow with a little gutta, and use this to paint the centre of the flower. Moisten the petals, then apply a little dilute purple mix round the yellow centre to leave a wide band of cream.

Pansy 2 Paint the flower centre as pansy 1. Use a fine brush to apply a narrow band of clear gutta round the outer edges of the petals and leave to dry. Moisten the petals with water and paint them with a blue/purple mix.

Pansy 3 Paint the flower centre as pansy 1. Mix deep purple with gutta, apply a band of this mix round the petals as shown and leave to dry. Finally, use the yellow/gutta mix to colour the remaining parts of the petals.

Pansy 4 Use the yellow/gutta mix to paint a large, streaked centre. Mix a very deep purple and apply this to the edge of the petals, allowing it to bleed down to the centre.

Pansy 5 Moisten the petals, then apply a dilute, pale blue colour, allowing it to fade into the centre of the flower. Use the yellow/gutta mix to paint the flower centre, then use the deep purple/gutta mix to apply a band of colour round the middle of each petal as shown.

8. When all the flowers are completely dry, cut the base ribbon, 1cm either side of each pansy, fold under the base ribbon and sew each pansy to the background.

Water lilies and bullrushes

The simplicity of the design makes this picture so attractive. I used the random painting technique on the silk background to suggest water.

I then used centre ribbon stitch and white ribbon to work the water lilies; I worked the base petals first, then continued working round the flower, adding more layers of petals to fill the centre. I used pale pink paint to shade the lily. Moistening one petal at a time, I applied the paint at the base and allowed it to fade out to the edge. I used two strands of yellow thread to work a cluster of twisted stamens (see page 20) to complete the lily.

Each bullrush is a 20cm gathered length of ribbon with the stitches running through the centre of the ribbon. All the leaves are straight stitch, controlled over a needle. The bent leaves are secured at the point of the bend with toning thread.

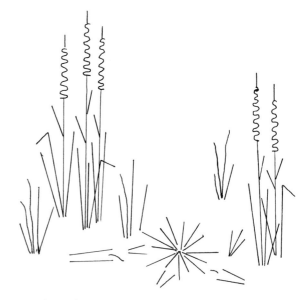

Enlarge this diagram to 150% for a full-size template.

You will need

Fabric
20cm square of silk habotai

Ribbons
66cm of 7mm white (03)
66cm of 7mm deep green (21)
1.5m of 4mm gold (54)
1.5m of 2mm moss green (20)

Silk paints
Blue and magenta

Threads
Toning threads including yellow for the stamens

Magnolia

I can see this magnolia from my workroom and it is so beautiful when it is in full bloom. I applied a pale green, fabric paint wash to the evenweave fabric, and used two shades of brown to colour the piece of muslin. When the muslin was dry, I cut it to make two 3 x 20cm lengths, twisted each length to form the branch and couched it to the painted background with a toning thread. The magnolia petals are worked in numerical order, using the ribbon stitches marked on the template. A touch of colour is applied at the base of each petal in a similar way to that used for the lily opposite. The calyxes for each flower are also ribbon stitches worked in 4mm khaki ribbon.

You will need

Fabric
25 x 20cm piece of linen/cotton evenweave

6 x 20cm piece of muslin, cut on the cross

Ribbon
1.5m of 13mm white (03)
66cm of 4mm khaki (56)

Fabric paints
blue, yellow and red

Silk paints
Magenta and blue

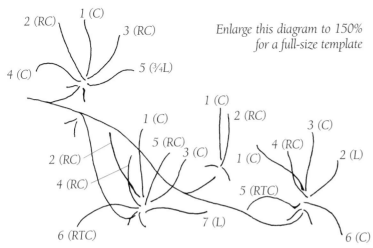

Enlarge this diagram to 150% for a full-size template

C   centre ribbon stitch
RC   reversed centre ribbon stitch
L   left-hand ribbon stitch
RTC ribbon turned, then centre ribbon stitch
¾L   ¼ distance from left-hand edge

Flower containers

A container for your silk ribbon flowers can make all the difference to a design. Here are just a few shapes for you to try. I make a habit of collecting interesting fabrics and threads; they always prove useful and often inspire particular designs.

Textured pot

Lots of different colours, thicknesses and types of threads have been used to create the textured surface of this pot.

1. Use the template to transfer the outline of the vase on to the fabric.

2. Combine long lengths of different threads together, take the ends through to the back and secure.

3. On the front, twist these threads and couch them to the fabric with toning thread, swirling them about to create the textured surface.

4. Use fabric paints to add the shadows.

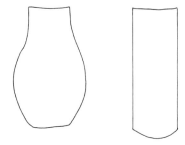

Enlarge these diagrams to 200% for full-size templates

This pot is featured in the embroidery on page 77.

This vase is featured in the embroidery on page 65.

Vase

This vase is quite easy to create. I used background fabric, a 3 x 8cm piece of wadding, a 10cm square of linen and a 5cm square of blue cotton fabric.

1. Use a craft knife to cut round the template. Retain both the template and the cut out shape.

2. Pin the template to the background and lightly draw round the shape with a pencil. Remove the template.

3. Use the cut out shape to cut the wadding to the same size. Place the wadding on the background within the pencilled outline and tack it down with a few stitches.

4. Use the cut out shape to cut the linen 1cm oversize on both sides and the bottom. Align the top of the linen with that of the wadding, then tack this down with a few stitches.

5. Working from the top of one of the sides, and working a small area at a time to prevent puckering, turn the linen under the wadding and slip stitch the edge of this hem so that it just covers the pencilled outline.

6. Oversew the top edges of the linen and wadding.

7. Using two strands of blue thread work two parallel rows of small running stitches down and across the linen as decoration.

8. Cut the blue fabric across the diagonal, and fringe the two short sides. Hem 5mm of the long side, and secure with thread.

Cut-glass bowl

This bowl consists of a 15cm square of white silk habotai, a small piece of wadding and a few clear glass beads.

1. Referring to steps 1–6 for the vase, attach the wadding and silk to the background fabric.

2. Mix shades of pale green, blue and a pinky mauve with the silk paints. Moisten the silk with clean water then colour the bowl, using a hairdryer to prevent the colours from seeping on to the background fabric.

3. Now, with a lightly-loaded brush, paint the shadow on the background fabric. Leave to dry.

4. Use one strand of white thread to work a row of back stitches just above the base of the bowl. Use the same thread to work a series of evenly spaced straight stitches diagonally across the fabric as shown on the template.

5. Sew a clear glass bead at each intersection of the diagonal straight stitches to pull the silk down on to the background fabric.

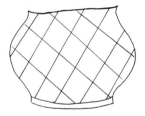

Enlarge this diagram to 200% for a full-size template.

Basket

This basket can be adapted to make different shapes. It is created with just 3m each of soft beige and brown six-stranded threads.

1. Thread six strands of the dark thread into a needle and knot one end. Bring the needle up at point A, then take it down at B to create the first upright. Bring it up at C and down at D, then continue across the design until the other uprights have been worked. Fasten off.

2. Now thread a 1.5m length of both colours (twelve strands) on to the needle and knot one end. Bring the threads up at point E, then use the eye of the needle to weave these threads over and under the vertical stitches. Use a pin at point F to keep the angle, then continue weaving the side of the basket, taking the thread down through the fabric at the end of the row. Bring the threads up again close to the first row, then work back across to the right-hand side of the basket. Continue weaving until the sides of the basket are complete.

3. Use the stab stitch technique to work a row of back stitches across the bottom edge of the basket to form the rolled bottom edge.

4. Divide the strands into two lengths, each with three strands of both colours, and bring each of these up at points G and H. Twist both threads together at point I, then couch the combined thread to the shape of the handle. Take the thread through to the back then fasten off.

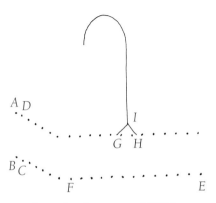

Enlarge this diagram to 200% for a full-size template.

This vase is featured in the embroidery on page 67.

This basket is featured in the embroidery on page 79.

Painting ribbons

Although silk ribbons come in a wide range of colours, a little silk paint will add a whole new dimension to your embroidery. You will be able to choose an exact colour to shade or alter the tone of a flower. You can paint the ribbons before embroidering with them or you can complete a design, then add touches of colour to the embroidered ribbons.

Delphiniums and asters

Delphiniums show tones to great effect so this design is ideal for shaded ribbons. I mixed two mauves from blue and magenta silk paints, then shaded light pink and blue ribbon.

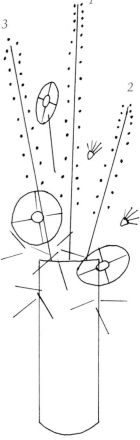

Enlarge this diagram to 150% for a full-size pattern.

> **You will need**
>
> **Fabric**
> 26 x 37cm of silk noile for the background, and the fabrics for the vase and cloth (see page 62)
>
> **Ribbons**
> 1.5m of 7mm, pink (08)
> 1.5m of 7mm and 33cm of 4mm mid blue (126)
> 66cm of 7mm deep green (21)
> 66cm of 7mm moss green (20)
> 3m of 2mm deep pink (128)
>
> **Threads**
> Green coton à broder for the stems and a range of toning stranded threads including two yellows
>
> **Silk paints** Magenta and blue

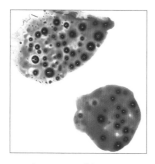

1. Place some blue and magenta paint on opposite corners of the palette, then add touches of each colour to the other to mix two shades of mauve.

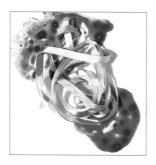

2. Drop in the lengths of dry pink and blue ribbon.

3. Use a stiff brush to push and swirl the ribbon into the colours so that they take up all the paint. Add a drop of clean water to any dry areas. Use pegs to hang the ribbon up to dry, then press with a medium hot iron.

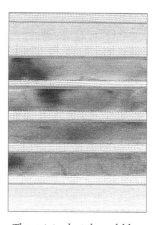

The original pink and blue ribbons (top and bottom), together with lengths of shaded ribbon.

Embroidering the design

Prepare the vase (see page 62), then using coton à broder work straight stitch stems as shown on the template opposite. The three delphiniums are a variation of those shown on page 22, in that the florets on the lower half of each flower are worked with gathered ribbon (see page 34). I used shaded blue ribbon for flowers 1 and 2, and shaded pink for flower 3.

1. For flower 3 prepare a 33cm length of 7mm ribbon as shown on page 34, then anchor the knotted end at point A. Gather 2 – 2.5cm of the ribbon nearest the fabric, shape this into a small circle and stab stitch the centre in place. Thread the other end of the ribbon into a needle and take it through to the back at point A. Bring the needle up at the next nearest point (dot) on the other side of the stem, gather another short length, form a floret and stab stitch this in position. Continue working up the stem, from side to side, until the ribbon is used up, then fasten off.

2. To finish flower 1 use another length of the same colour 7mm ribbon to work straight-stitch loops (see page 22) for the other florets (make each one a little smaller as you work up the stem). Stop a short distance from the top, then use the 4mm shaded ribbon to work a few tiny straight stitch buds.

3. Use two strands of thread to work a two-loop French knot (see page 28) in the centre of each floret.

4. Work flower 2 in the same way then work flower 3 with the painted pink ribbon, but omit the tiny buds at the top.

5. For the asters use the 2mm deep pink ribbon to work straight-stitch petals (see page 19). Use two strands of yellow thread and one-loop French knots to fill the centre of each flowerhead.

6. Finally, use both shades of the 7mm green ribbon to form the straight-stitch leaves.

The finished embroidery

The beautiful tall delphiniums complement their slender container and the deep pink asters add a vibrant splash of colour.

Sweet peas

These sweet peas look as though they have just been brought in from the garden and simply placed in a cut glass bowl – they look so real that you can almost smell them. Their subtle shades of colour and variegated form are the perfect subject for a controlled application of paint. I used yellow, blue and red silk paints to mix tones of green for the leaves, and magenta and red to mix three pinks for the flowers.

You will need

Fabric
35cm square of linen/cotton evenweave, and fabric for the vase (see page 63)

Ribbons
3m of 13mm white (03)
3m of 13mm cream (156)
1.3m of 7mm white (03)
33cm of 4mm moss green (20)

Threads
3m of moss green coton à broder for the stems and toning stranded thread.

Silk paints
Red, magenta, yellow and blue

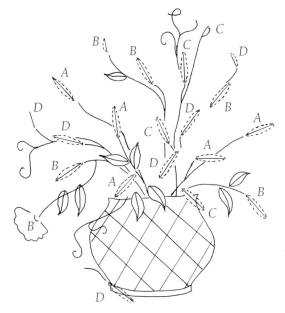

Enlarge this diagram to 200% for a full-size template.

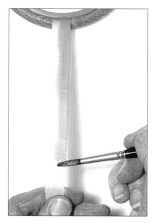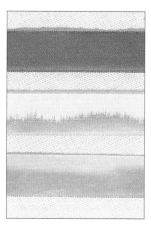

Secure one end of a length of ribbon in a hoop, then, holding the ribbon taut, moisten the entire length with clean water. Apply the paint evenly across the width (left), just along the selvedge (centre), or half way across (right). Dry the ribbon by suspending it from the hoop or a clothes peg. Do not hang the ribbon over a bar.

The painted ribbons.

Tips

Limit the number of colours you use; too many contrasting colours can spoil the finished work.

Mix and paint with one colour at a time.

Use a plastic hoop, weighted one side, to anchor ribbons when painting them. It is easy to wipe clean.

Tip

When working a flower with two lengths of painted ribbon, cut both lengths consecutively so that they are the same tone, and pin them together until you are ready to stitch the flower.

Preparing the ribbons

1. Cut the lengths of 13mm, white and cream ribbon in half. Set one cream length aside for flowers D.

2. Mix a little magenta and red paint with water to make a mid-rose pink; paint across the whole width of one of the lengths of white ribbon. Use this ribbon for flowers A on the pattern opposite.

3. Use the same colour to paint a length of cream ribbon, but, this time only take the paint halfway across the width. Use this for flowers B.

4. Mix magenta paint with water to create a medium pink, then paint just the selvedge of the second length of white ribbon. Use this for flowers C.

5. Cut the 7mm white ribbon in half, mix yellow and blue silk paints with a touch of red to make two shades of moss green, then paint the whole width of the ribbon as shown opposite. When dry, press the ribbon with a medium hot iron.

Preparing the background

1. Lightly draw in the shape of the bowl on to the background fabric.

2. Use yellow and blue silk paint to mix a few shades of pale green, moisten the fabric with clean water then paint areas of the fabric so that the colours run into each other. Do not paint a shadow behind the bowl.

3. Now mix two slightly deeper shades of green, then sponge these behind where the flowers are to be embroidered.

4. Dry the fabric then press with an iron to fix the colours.

5. Prepare the glass bowl as described on page 63.

Embroidering the flowers

All the outer petals are worked with 9cm gathered lengths of ribbon. However, the flower centres vary in size, so also gather ribbon lengths of 5.5, 6 and 7cm. Use the shorter lengths for the flowers with the less open centres at the top of the design. Some lower flowers hang down, so take care to place them correctly.

1. Referring to the instructions on page 41, and the template opposite, transfer the straight lines for each flower on to the fabric and embroider the flowers.

2. Use one strand of toning thread to couch two twisted strands of coton à broder for the stems and one strand for the tendrils.

3. Work the leaves in ribbon stitch using the darker tones of 7mm green ribbon for those in shadow.

4. Use the 4mm moss green ribbon and two small ribbon stitches for the calyx at the base of each bud.

Californian poppies

For this project all the flowers are embroidered with white ribbon and then painted *in situ*. Each flower is moistened with clean water and then painted with a round, pointed brush. Californian poppies come in so many glorious colours you will really be able to experiment. You can use my range of colours, which were mixed from yellow, blue and magenta silk paints, or choose your own colour scheme. The background is sponged with shades of green.

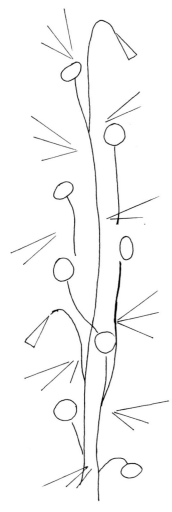

Enlarge this diagram to 150% for a full-size template.

You will need

Fabric
28 x 40cm piece of calico

Ribbon
1.66m of 13mm white (03)
1.33m of 7mm moss green (20)
66cm of 7mm deep moss green (72)
1m of 2mm moss green (20)

Threads
Various stranded threads including some greens, and white, black and yellow

Fabric paints
Blue, yellow and red

Silk paints
Magenta, yellow, blue

Preparing the background

1. Tack round the outside edges of the design, then draw in the flower centres and centre lines of both buds.

2. Mix two shades of green from blue and yellow silk paint with a touch of red, moisten the fabric, then wash these over the whole surface, allowing the colours to blend. Leave to dry.

3. Mix two more greens, moisten a sponge, pick up some colour and lightly sponge the background behind where the flowers are to be worked. Leave to dry.

4. Referring to the instructions on page 37, use one strand of white thread and the white ribbon to embroider the open poppies.

5. Form each bud with a single straight stitch worked from the stem end to the tip.

Tip

Dab a loaded brush on paper towel to remove any excess moisture before starting to paint. This will prevent excess paint dropping on to the fabric or, more importantly, causing the colour to seep into the fabric.

If the ribbon does become too wet and colours start to seep on to the background, use a hairdryer to dry the fabric quickly.

Painting the flowers

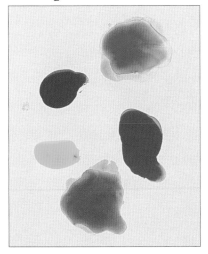

1. Prepare the colours. Mix the magenta on a tile with a little water to make pink. Mix red with a spot of yellow for the red flowers; add a little more yellow and dilute with water for the softer orange.

2. Place a paper towel under the flower to be painted and moisten the ribbon with clean water. The paper towel protects the background fabric.

3. Remove the paper towel, but keep it close so that you can remove excess liquid from the brush. For this flower, which has just a tinge of colour on the outside of the petals, apply the pink paint to the selvedge and allow it to fade out towards the centre.

4. For flowers with a more intense, graded tone, work as before but take the brush a little further down the petal. Darken the pink slightly and apply more paint to the selvedge to create more tone.

5. The top flower is painted with the orange shade. Here I allowed the colour to spread right across the width of the ribbon, then I used a hairdryer to stop the colour from seeping into the background fabric.

6. Mix blue and yellow with a spot of red to make a deep olive green then add a drop of gutta on to the tile.

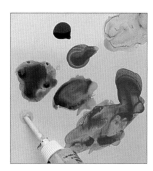

7. Mix this green into the gutta, then paint round the centre of the red flowers. The gutta restricts the movement of the colour, allowing you to add fine detail.

Finishing the embroidery

1. Draw in the stems. Using 7mm moss green ribbon, work a fairly loose straight stitch across the centre of each poppy. Then, using one strand of black thread for the red poppies and yellow for the others, work two-loop French knots round the inner edge of the petals taking a few through the green centre to secure it.

2. Knot together the ends of a length of 2mm moss green ribbon and two strands of toning thread. Twisting the ribbon/thread as you work, couch a stem for each flower.

3. Use the 7mm moss green ribbon to work a straight stitch on either side of each bud, taking the ribbon over a second needle to sit the calyx round the bud.

4. Embroider the leaves in ribbon stitch with 7mm deep moss and moss green ribbons (see also leaf 4 on page 46). Work the long stitch first, then overlap two shorter stitches on the lower side. Complete each leaf with six strands of toning green thread; work a long stitch three quarters of the way along the top edge of the first ribbon stitch, then a few shorter ones to mirror the shape of the ribbon-part of the leaf.

Single rose

This beautiful rose with its gently curling petals was embroidered with 13mm pale cream ribbon. Each petal is carefully placed and the rose completed before being lightly painted in a lovely pale apricot.

Enlarge this diagram to 125% for a full-size template.

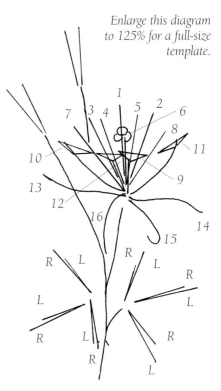

You will need

Fabric
27 x 30cm piece of linen/cotton evenweave

Ribbon
2m of 13mm cream (156)
66cm of 7mm moss green (20)
66cm of 7mm deep green (21)
66cm of 4mm deep green (21)

Threads
Three shades (pale to mid green) coton à broder and a selection of toning embroidery threads

Silk paint
red and yellow

This embroidery is shown full size on page 3.

1. Mark the positions of just the petal tips and refer to the template to position the base of each petal, (any marks for the base point will be covered as you stitch).

2. Anchor the cream ribbon at the base of petal 1; work a reverse centre ribbon stitch for petals 1, 2 and 3; work slightly more rounded stitches for petals 4 and 5. Fasten off.

3. For petal 6 anchor another length of ribbon and work a two-loop French knot (see page 31, step 2) but do not take the needle down through the ribbon. The knot may be tilted to sit properly with one strand of toning thread and a small stitch.

4. Make a left ribbon stitch for petal 7, taking the needle down midway between the centre of the ribbon and the selvedge. Work petal 8 in a similar manner, but with a right ribbon stitch.

5. Work a centre ribbon stitch for petal 9, holding the second needle parallel to the top of the triangle.

Work petals 10, 11 and 12 in a similar manner, but with left, right and left ribbon stitches respectively.

6. For the four front petals, 13–16, lay the ribbon round the base of the rose and work reverse centre ribbon stitches with gentle rolls.

7. Anchor the ribbon at the base of a bud, then work the left-hand petal with a left ribbon stitch, taking the needle down through the left selvedge. For the other petal, lay the ribbon over the first stitch and work a right ribbon stitch, so that the two rolled petals overlap. Fasten off.

8. Use a toning thread to couch a straight stitch stem (worked with three twisted, green coton à broder threads) in position.

9. Use the 7mm green ribbons (to suggest light and shade) to work the leaves, as in example 2 on page 46.

10. Use 4mm deep green ribbon to work a calyx of three ribbon stitches for each bud.

11. Mix a little red and yellow paint to make apricot. Using the eye of a needle to keep the petals apart, moisten petals 1–3 with a touch of water, then brush a little paint into the centre and allow it to fade out to the tip. Dry before working the next layer of petals. Use a deeper tone to paint the centre knot and the base of each bud.

Tip
Use a second needle to control the ribbon at the back of the work to prevent twisting and excess bulk. However when working a life-size flower, with numerous petals, it is often more practical (and easier) to anchor each stitch off. This practice saves taking a long length of ribbon across the back of the fabric to work the next petal.

Fuchsia sampler

This sampler of life-size fuchsias shows just a few of the many varieties there are (see pages 73 and 76). Each flower has been worked by developing the basic techniques shown on previous pages.

The embroidery was worked on a 37cm square of linen/cotton evenweave. Mark the position and embroider the flower first before adding the stem and leaves. Complete each fuchsia before moving on to the next.

Enlarge this diagram to 150% for full-size templates.

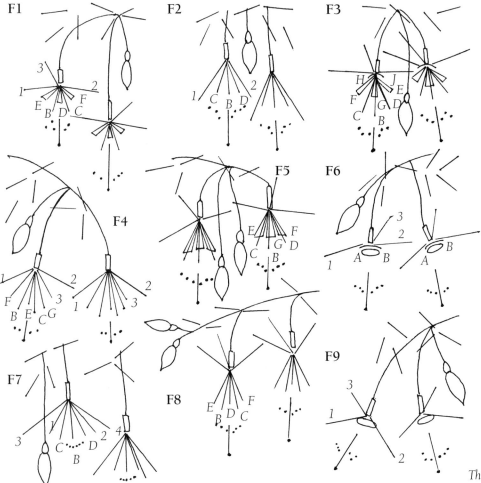

The instructions for each of these templates are on pages 73–76.

Basic fuchsia

The following instructions are an introduction to embroidering fuchsias. Read these notes in conjuction with the instructions for the different varieties (see overleaf). The template gives the numerical/alphabetical order in which the stitches should be worked. Before you start, mark the base petals on the background fabric.

1. Anchor the 7mm ribbon at point A, work the base petals B and C, the top petals D, E and F, then fasten off. Refer to specific instructions for stitches used.

2. Leave a 2mm space above point A, then, using 4mm ribbon (the same colour as the sepals) work a straight-stitch tube. Fasten off.

3. Use 7mm ribbon to work the sepals 1, 2 and 3 with left-, right- and centre-ribbon stitch respectively; make these slightly longer than the petals and allow the ribbon to twist for some.

4. Use one strand of thread and straight stitch for the stamens, and one or two for the stigma, then end each with a French knot. Note the colour of these knots.

5. The buds are straight stitches, worked with 7mm ribbon from stem to tip and couched with a toning thread.

6. The stem is a coton à broder straight stitch couched along the curve with one strand of toning embroidery thread.

7. The leaves are worked at random in ribbon stitch.

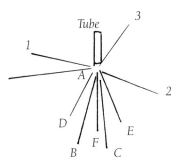

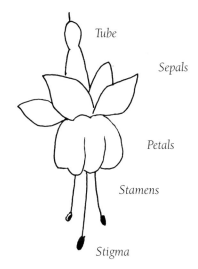

Blue Pearl (F1)

You will need
Ribbons
66cm of 7mm pale pink (05), painted with blue to make lilac
66cm of 7mm pink (08)
50cm of 7mm deep green (21)
25cm of 4mm pink (08)
Threads
Green and white coton à broder and white, pink and green stranded thread

Tip

It is important to use the eye of a second needle to position each petal to create the oval skirt for each flower.

1. Work two straight-stitch base petals B and C.

2. Bring the ribbon up at A and work a looped ribbon stitch at D taking the needle down through both the ribbon and fabric to give a more flared effect. Now work E and F, and fasten off.

3. Work the tube with 4mm pink ribbon and the sepals with 7mm pink ribbon.

4. Work one-loop French knots, using two strands of white thread for the stigma and one strand of pink for the stamens.

5. Work a single straight stitch bud, then add the stem and leaves.

Hampshire Treasure (F2)

Royal Velvet (F3)

Phyllis (F4)

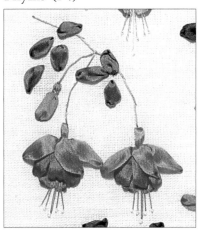

You will need

Ribbons

66cm of 7mm (40) orange
(painted red)
66cm of 7mm (167) apricot
50cm of 7mm (72) deep moss
25cm of 4mm (167) apricot

Threads

Green and white coton à
broder and white, orange and
green stranded thread

You will need

Ribbons

66cm of 7mm (02) red
66cm of 7mm (177) purple
50cm of 7mm (33) soft green
25cm of 4mm (02) red

Threads

Green and white coton à broder
and white, red and green
stranded thread

You will need

Ribbons

66cm of 7mm (112) deep
    salmon
66cm of 7mm (25) bright pink
50cm of 7mm (20) moss green
25cm of 4mm (112) deep
    salmon

Threads

Green coton à broder, and
white, pink and green
stranded thread

1. Paint the 7mm orange ribbon a deeper tone with a little diluted red paint. Use this ribbon to work a straight stitch base petal to B and then the two top petals C and D.

2. Use the 4mm apricot ribbon to work the straight stitch tube.

3. Use 7mm apricot ribbon to work the sepals 1 and 2. Flatten the ribbon and, without using a second needle, work a reverse ribbon stitch (see page 26, steps 1-4), pulling the ribbon away from A to elongate the stitch.

4. Use two strands of white thread for the stigma and one apricot for the stamens.

5. Work a single straight stitch bud, then add the stem and leaves.

1. Use the 7mm purple ribbon to work the straight stitch base petals B, C and D from the centre of line H– J. Now work three ribbon stitch loops (as for Blue Pearl) at E, F and G, then fasten off.

2. Gather a 6cm length of the 7mm purple ribbon, anchor the knot end at H and the other end at J, pull up gathering thread and stab stitch in a curve H–J.

3. Use 4mm red ribbon for the tube and 7mm red for the sepals.

4. Work the stamens and stigma in red with a white French knot for the stigma.

5. Work a single straight stitch bud, then add the stem and leaves.

1. Use the 7mm bright pink ribbon to work the straight stitch base petals B and C, then the three top petals D, E and F.

2. Work the tube with 4mm deep salmon ribbon and the sepals 1, 2 and 3 in 7mm salmon ribbon.

3. Work the stigma and stamens in pink thread with a white French knot.

4. Work a single straight stitch bud, then add the stem and leaves.

Collingwood (F5)

Marcus Graham (F6)

Rough Silk (F7)

You will need

Ribbons
75cm of 7mm (03) white
66cm of 7mm (24) mid pink
33cm of 7mm (21) deep green
25cm of 4mm (24) mid pink

Threads
Green coton à broder, and
white, pink and green
stranded thread

You will need

Ribbons
66cm of 7mm (112) deep
salmon
66cm of 7mm (05) pale pink
50cm of 7mm (72) deep moss
green
25cm of 4mm (05) pale pink

Threads
Green coton à broder, and
white, apricot and green
stranded thread

You will need

Ribbons
66cm of 7mm (114) dusky red
66cm of 7mm (05) pale pink
33cm of 7mm (21) deep green
25cm of 4mm (05) pale pink

Threads
Green coton à broder, and
white, red and green
stranded thread

1. Use the 7mm white ribbon to work the three straight stitch base petals B, C and D. Now, noting the angles of the petals, work E, F and G in ribbon stitch loops (as Blue Pearl, but longer). Bring a strand of white thread up at one side of petal E, pass the eye end of the needle through the loops of E, G and F and then down through the fabric at F; gently pull the thread to place the top petals. Fasten off.

2. Work the tube with 4mm mid pink and the sepals 1, 2 and 3 in 7mm mid pink ribbon.

3. Work the stigma in white thread and the stamens in pink.

4. Work a single straight stitch bud, then add the stem and leaves.

1. Draw the oval centres on the fabric.

2. Gather an 11cm length of 7mm deep salmon ribbon, anchor the end on the oval line and gather the ribbon as for the aquilegia (see page 40), then fasten off.

3. Gather a 5cm length of the same ribbon and stab stitch to curve A–B (as Royal Velvet).

4. Use 4mm pale pink for the tube and 7mm pale pink ribbon for the sepals.

5. Work the stigma in white thread and the stamens in pale apricot.

6. Work a single straight stitch bud, then add the stem and leaves.

1. Use the 7mm dusky red ribbon to work a reverse ribbon stitch (over a needle) for base petal B, an ordinary left ribbon stitch at C and a right ribbon stitch at D. Fasten off.

2. Work the tube with 4mm pale pink ribbon.

3. Use the 7mm pale pink ribbon to work a folded ribbon stitch for sepals 1 and 2. Now work an ordinary left ribbon stitch at 3 and right ribbon stitch at 4. Fasten off. Sepals on the lower flower are a left, right and centre ribbon stitch.

4. Work a short stigma and stamens in a toning red thread and add a white French knot.

5. Work a single straight stitch bud, then add the stem and leaves.

Northumberland Bell (F8)

Quaser (F9)

You will need

Ribbons
66cm of 7mm (44) pale blue
(painted red to mauve)
66cm of 7mm (25) bright pink
33cm of 7mm (33) soft green
25cm of 4mm (91) rose pink

Threads
Green coton à broder, and
white, pink and green
stranded thread

You will need

Ribbons
66cm of 7mm (178) pale
mauve
66cm of 7mm (03) white
33cm of 7mm (21) deep green
25cm of 4mm (03) white

Threads
Green coton à broder, and
white, mauve and green
stranded thread

1. Use red to shade the pale blue ribbon to soft purple (see Blue Pearl), then iron fix. Use this ribbon to work the straight stitch base petals B and C, a centre ribbon stitch at D, a left ribbon stitch at E and a right ribbon stitch at F. Fasten off.

2. Work the tube with 4mm wide rose pink ribbon and the sepals with 7mm bright pink.

3. Work a white French knot for the stigma, then work the stamens in a toning pink thread.

4. Work two straight stitch buds, then add the stem and leaves.

1. Draw the oval centres on the fabric. Gather a 13cm length of pale mauve ribbon (as for the poppies on page 37, but placing the vertical stitches 1.5cm apart).

2. Anchor and gather the ribbon (as for the aquilegia on page 40), then fasten off.

3. Work the tube with 4mm white ribbon and the sepals with 7mm white.

4. Work the stigma in white thread and the stamens in pale mauve.

5. Work a single straight stitch bud, then add the stem and leaves.

Chinese lanterns

The dried cow parsley in this composition, contrasts perfectly with the vibrant, stark shape of the dried Chinese lanterns, their painted leaves and the coarse textured pot.

This embroidery is featured full size on page 1.

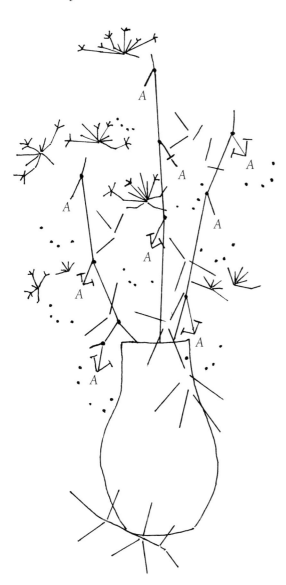

Enlarge this diagram to 125% for a full-size template.

You will need
Fabric
28 x 35cm of ivory silk noile
Ribbons
2.3m of 7mm orange (40)
2m of 7mm white (03)
Threads
A selection of toning threads, including sand, gold and silver and those required for the pot (see page 62)
Silk paint
Blue, yellow and red

1. Prepare the pot as shown on page 62.

2. Use two strands of gold thread to work straight stitch stems for the cow parsley then one strand to work fly stitches for the umbrella top.

3. Use one strand of silver thread and four strands of sand thread to work a straight stitch from the vase to the top of the Chinese lantern stem, then working downwards make a one-loop French knot at each notch to kink the stem.

4. Mark the position of each flower. Anchor the ribbon at point A, then, using a second needle, work the very rounded centre ribbon stitches, followed by a left and right ribbon stitch on either side. Position the straight stitches with care.

5. Mix blue, yellow and red paint to make shades of green, khaki and brown, then drop the ribbon in the paint for the leaves (see page 64). Mix a brown/grey colour, then use a small stiff brush to paint the vase shadow; dry and iron fix.

6. Work the stem at the base of the vase, add the ribbon stitch leaves, then work the leaves in the vase. Add the other stems.

7. Use tiny pieces of cotton wool under the petals to help retain their shape.

Spray of chrysanthemums

Straight and ribbon stitches are used to create the flowers and leaves in this design. The fullness of each flower is created by working three rounds of petals, mostly in straight stitch but with some ribbon stitches. Keep the tension fairly loose and allow some petals to twist. Work each petal from the centre out to the tip, and always control the ribbon over a second needle.

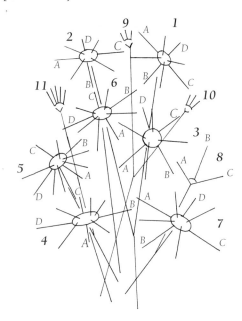

This embroidery is featured full size on page 7.

Enlarge this diagram to 200% for a full-size pattern. Embroider the flowers and buds in numerical order, and work petals A–D first. The other marked petals define the overall shape of each flower.

You will need

Fabric
30 x 32cm linen/cotton evenweave

Fabric paints
yellow, blue and touches of red mixed to create three shades of pale green

Threads
2m of size 16, moss green coton à broder thread for the stems and toning stranded embroidery threads

Ribbons
2m of 4mm corn (35) for flower 1 and buds 9 and 10
4.66m of 4mm copper (109) for flowers 2, 3 and 4
1.66m of 4mm spice (55) for flower 5 and bud 11
3m of 2mm deep yellow (15) for flowers 6, 7 and 8
1m each of 4mm and 7mm soft green (33) for the leaves
66cm of 2mm soft green (33) for the calyx

---

1. Referring to pages 52 to 55, use the three shades of green to paint a wash across the fabric allowing the colours to mix. Dry and iron fix.

2. Mark the positions of the stems on the fabric, then use two threads of twisted coton à broder for the flower stems, and one thread for the bud stems. Use one strand of a toning embroidery thread to couch each stem in place.

3. Mark the centre shape of each flower and the positions of their petals on the fabric.

4. Working with the 4mm ribbon colours listed above, embroider flowers 1–5. Embroider petals A, B, C and D in straight stitch. Work three more rounds of petals inside the previous round, making the centre a little smaller each time. Work some petals in ribbon stitch and allow some of the stitches to twist. Dome the centre of each flower with straight stitch loops worked closely together.

5. Embroider flowers 6–8 with 2mm deep yellow ribbon. Build up rounds of petals as described in step 4, twisting each stitch as for the bergamot on page 21.

6. Working with the 4mm ribbon colours listed above, embroider buds 9–11 and each calyx in ribbon stitch.

7. Embroider the leaves with 4mm and 7mm ribbon dependent on their size. Use three ribbon stitches for each leaf – a long centre ribbon stitch, with a short one either side.

Polyanthus and daffodils

This embroidery is shown full size on page 23.

You will need

Fabric
20cm square of cotton/linen evenweave

Basket
See list on page 63

Ribbons
66cm of 2mm deep yellow (15)
66cm of 4mm deep yellow (15)
66cm of 4mm delph blue (117)
66cm of 4mm violet (118)
33cm of 4mm yellow (13)
33cm of 4mm dusky red (114)
33cm of 4mm deep red (50)

33cm of 4mm deep salmon (112)
33cm of 4mm pink (08)
66cm of 4mm soft orange (16)
33cm of 4mm spice (55)
33cm of 2mm deep green (21)
66cm of 7mm deep green (21)
66cm of 7mm moss green (20)
33cm of 2mm soft green (33)
33cm of 2mm khaki (56)

Threads
Toning threads for anchoring ribbons, and various green threads for stems and veins

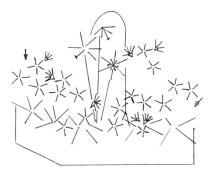

Enlarge this diagram to 200% for a full-size template.

1. Create the basket as shown on page 63, then paint the leafy background and the shadow on the fabric (see page 52).

2. Use straight stitches for all the flower petals, working them from the flower centre out to their tips.

3. Use various green ribbons for the leaves.

4. Use one strand of toning thread and straight stitches to create veins on some of the foreground leaves; then use a variety of green threads for the stems.

Group of irises

This little group or irises are all worked in lazy daisy stitch (see page 42). The leaves are worked in straight stitch (see page 18).

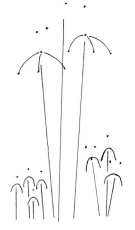

Enlarge this diagram to 200% for a full-size template.

You will need

Fabric
18 x 24cm, linen/cotton evenweave

Ribbons
33cm of 7mm cream (156)
33cm of 7mm deep yellow (15)
33cm of 4mm khaki (56)
66cm of 4mm soft green (33)
66cm of 4mm just green (61)
33cm of 4mm delph blue (117)
33cm of 4mm violet (118)
33cm of 4mm mid blue (126)
33cm of 4mm blue (45)
66cm of 2mm deep green (21)

Threads
A variety of toning threads

Fabric paints
Blue and yellow

This embroidery also appears on page 43.

1. Use two tones of 7mm ribbon for the group of large flowers, and two tones of 4mm ribbon for each group of small flowers.

2. Use the 7mm deep yellow and 4mm khaki to work three straight stitches for the bud.

3. Use two strands of thread for the straight stitch stems, then the 2 and 4mm green ribbons for the leaves.

4. Finally, use fabric paint to give an indication of water at the base.

Index